NEVER FORGET
OUR PEOPLE
WERE ALWAYS FREE

Also by Ben Jealous

Reach: 40 Black Men Speak on Living, Leading, and Succeeding

. . . and edited by his mother, Ann Todd Jealous, with Caroline T. Haskell

Combined Destinies: Whites Sharing Grief About Racism

NEVER FORGET OUR PEOPLE WERE ALWAYS FREE

A Parable of American Healing

Ben Jealous

AMISTAD

An Imprint of HarperCollins*Publishers*

Some names were changed to protect identities of the innocent and the guilty. In each case, only a first name was used, never a last name.

HarperCollins books may be purchased for educational, business, or sales promotional use. For information, please email the Special Markets Department at SPsales@harpercollins.com.

FIRST EDITION

Designed by Elina Cohen

Cover illustration: © Zoltan Toth, Trevillion Images, 17th-century slave ship on Virginia's James River

Library of Congress Cataloging-in-Publication Data has been applied for.

ISBN 978-0-06-296174-7

23 24 25 26 27 LBC 5 4 3 2 1

To Jack, Morgan, Emma, Dylan, and Nina

CONTENTS

HEY, COUSIN!

A news alert flashed on one of the screens: *VP Cheney Rushed to Hospital.*

We were on a commercial break. I was sitting at the table on NBC's Sunday morning talk show *Meet the Press*. It was 2013, and I was national president of the NAACP. I was there to discuss the case of yet another Black teenager who had been wrongfully killed.

I leaned over to the host, David Gregory, and confessed, "I just found out he's my cousin."

He looked at me and shrugged. "Isn't he, like, every Black person's cousin?"

I was stunned by his reply. Then I remembered that President Barack Obama and Vice President Dick Cheney were cousins too. He had a point.

"I'm pretty sure that's not how he thinks of himself," I said with a chuckle.

The show resumed.

Later, on the way home, I pondered the exchange. I remembered that Myrlie Evers, the widow of the slain NAACP leader Medgar Evers, had once told me she was pretty sure she and the former Arizona senator (and 2008 Republican nominee for president) John McCain were cousins. Other civil rights leaders who hailed from the South said they were cousins to him too. Some Black leaders were even kin to notorious segregationists. My grandma had told me about the White supremacist senator Strom Thurmond's Black daughter long before it was national news.

I decided a more fitting reply would've been "Aren't we all cousins?"

I couldn't help but wonder what would happen if every American actually acted like every other American was their cousin too.

My mind drifted back to my newfound cousin. The only time I had met Cheney, a Wyoming Republican who had spent his career in Congress before ascending to the vice presidency, was at President George W. Bush's last Fourth of July party as president. I was invited to the White House because I had just been appointed to my role at the NAACP. Cheney and I were dressed identically. At the time, it was a little awkward. My recent discovery that we had common ancestors in England made me wonder if a preference for lavender checked shirts was the product of shared genes.

TROUBLE IN THE AIR

They say we're headed toward a civil war.

Who is *they?* Historians, sociologists, television pundits, and the last guy with whom I had a real conversation at my favorite Jimmy Buffett–style waterside bar. He was an amiable older man wearing a T-shirt that celebrated his status as a veteran. Just past seventy, he'd spent half a century moving up the ranks in a grocery store. He and his wife approached where we were sitting before paying my date and I a compliment. We quickly fell into a warm conversation about life, kids, whiskey, and boats.

As we were preparing to leave, the conversation paused. The man looked at me and said, "You know, this country we both love so much? It's headed toward a civil war or a revolution, I don't know which."

The only difference between the two, of course, is who wins.

I honestly don't know what to make of it all.

What I can tell you is this: America needs a spiritual reckoning and an actual revival.

We think of ourselves as a nation that makes stuff. In the past thirty years, 63,000 factories have shuttered.

We think of ourselves as a free nation. We, Americans of all colors, are the most incarcerated people on the planet.

We are home to the most innovative healthcare system on the

planet. High healthcare costs have been our nation's leading cause of bankruptcy for decades.

We are home to many of the world's greatest universities. Millions upon millions of our students and graduates are in massive debt.

The life expectancy for Black men, like me and my son, remains too low, suppressed in large part by sky-high homicide rates.

The life expectancy of White men, like that man in the bar and my father, has been declining for years. It is driven by suicide rates that are even higher than the homicide rates for Black men and boys.

We no longer wonder why opiate addiction is out of control in the small towns and the big cities.

And yet, despite the sky-high tensions, despite surging gun sales, despite Americans of all colors dying from bullets all too often, I still remain optimistic about the future of our country. All of us—every American of every race, gender, creed, and color—must have faith that we can hand over a better, stronger nation to our children. It's our only path to national survival, let alone true greatness.

As the Bible reminds us, faith is hard to maintain. So as to ensure we get the lesson, the same definition of faith is repeated in both the Old and New Testaments: Faith is "the substance of things hoped for, and the evidence of things not seen."[1]

There is a reason "Amazing Grace" is our unofficial national anthem. We are each called to grapple honestly with the racial and political insanity into which we were born and heal our communities and ourselves. My life has taught me to realize that grace is as doable as it is urgent, for all of us and for the sake of all our children.

The more I think about the conversation in that bar, the more it occurs to me that the tensions in our nation have been building throughout this century. They surged after the terrorist attacks of 9/11. They surged after we elected Barack Hussein Obama president. They surged after we elected Donald John Trump president. They are surging now.

The first sign I got that we might be in more trouble than we realized was New Year's Eve 1999.

I traveled to Ohio to celebrate that night with my godbrother Dave Chappelle, my godfather's son. He was excited to show me his first home, a ranch house just outside Yellow Springs, Ohio, that he shared with his wife Elaine.

Dave invited me, his brother Yusuf, and his oldest friend, "Jamaican Marcus," to join him there. The ranch was on an old farm, surrounded by cornfields. The farm provided maximum privacy and a wonderful plot of land to explore. It was also situated between the universities where his father taught and his great-grandfather served as president: Antioch and Wilberforce.

I was excited to see it.

I should have known something was wrong when I arrived at the airport. In front of me in the security line was a man dressed for a cowboy-themed New Year's event. Every article of his clothing had steel on it—his cowboy boots, his spurs, his belt buckle, his belt tip, his collar weights, his bolo tie, the ribbon holder on the side of his hat, and even the fancy washers that held together the tassels on his jacket.

Back then, security at our airports wasn't generally so tight. The metal detectors were more of a formality. They normally didn't check ID. But Y2K had everything tighter than a drum.

Everyone from preachers to Prince was prophesizing about what might occur at the end of the millennium that night. Meanwhile, what had governments and corporations freaking out was an entirely different problem. Computers, of course, were a twentieth-century invention. As such, their codes ran on two-digit inputs for each year. January 1, 1999, was 01/01/99. That had never been a problem. However, at the start of a new millennium, there was concern that computers would think time had been turned back to January 1, 1900. If that happened, airplanes could disappear from radar screens, bank computers could crash, society could find itself suddenly plunged into chaos.

At the FBI and the CIA, there was concern that everyone from domestic gangs to international terrorists were prepared to exploit the moment. Meanwhile, most Americans simply wanted to party like it was 1999.

That night, IDs were being checked, everything was being scanned, and the metal detectors were set on high.

As I stood in the security line, I watched them all but strip the cowboy in front of me.

First, they had him take off his hat; then, the jacket; then, the bolo tie; then the shirt with the steel collar weights; next, the belt had to be removed; next, they pointed at his feet and told him to take off his boots. By the time they were done with him, the rail-thin rhinestone cowboy was half naked, stripped down to his tank top undershirt with one hand in the air and the other holding up his jeans.

This might seem routine now. It certainly wasn't back then. Even as everyone in line began to quietly calculate whether they would be able to make their flights, it was clear that they felt for him.

He was more than annoyed.

The cowboy's eyes focused on the security guard who had squatted down so he could run his wand through the cowboy's legs with precision.

The security officer appeared to be a very conscientious man of East African descent. The cowboy let him have it. "What? Do I look like some goddamn Arab terrorist?" The security guard kept going and glanced up. "No, sir," he said, still squatting, momentarily pausing his wand over the man's crotch. "Just Timothy McVeigh's cousin, sir."

Just a few years earlier, McVeigh had organized the deadliest domestic terrorist attack in American history. He and his accomplice, Terry Nichols, loaded a Ryder truck full of fertilizer, which they converted into a massive bomb. They deployed it at the Murrah Federal Building in Oklahoma City. In addition to housing hundreds of federal employees, it was home to a daycare center. When the bomb exploded, it killed 168 men, women, and children, and injured dozens more.

The killers were able to flee town easily, in part because local law enforcement officers were reportedly looking for Arab terrorists.

The security guard's retort landed. The New Year's Eve cowboy fell quiet.

When I arrived in Yellow Springs, Dave greeted me. His brother Yusuf and his childhood friend Marcus did too. Everyone was in high spirits. Time to celebrate. Time for the tour of the new house! Dave walked us through every room, making sure everything was perfect for the family to move in the next day. He worked through the checklist for the furnishings as we went: twin beds in the boys' room; a king-size bed in the master; a big, fancy remote for the new television; and on and on.

When he got to the end of the list, he cussed.

"Shit!"

"What, Dave?"

"Motherfucker didn't buy me that gun."

"Dave!"

"Yeah?"

"Motherfucker can't buy you that gun. You have to do that yourself. It requires a background check."

"Right! Come on, boys. We're going to buy a gun."

I was concerned. "Hold up. Why are we going to buy a gun?"

"Ben . . ." He took a deep breath and smiled beneficently. "Let's step outside."

I thought Dave wanted to explain to me why he wanted to buy a gun. In a way, I was right. He simply pointed across the road. "What do you see over there?"

"Cornfields," I responded flatly.

"And over there?"

"Cornfields," I replied again.

"And over there?"

"A cornfield," I said once again, a bit exasperated.

"How many niggas you think own them cornfields?" Dave asked, with finality.

"None," I replied.

"That is precisely correct, Ben. I don't know how it is right now back East, but out here, these evangelical preachers have been preaching that the war to end all wars comes tomorrow. The Apocalypse, Ben. Tomorrow.

"Tomorrow is not just the end of the year. It's not just the end of the decade. It's not just the end of the century. Ben, it's the end of the millennium. I don't know who's right, but I'll tell you this. If the worst ones are right, if tomorrow really is the race war to end all race wars, wouldn't you feel safer if we had a gun?"

I took a long pause before replying, "Do you even know how to shoot a gun?"

"No, but you do."

"I do."

"And you are going to train everybody to shoot tonight."

"Okay. You know that the only gun we can get on a moment's notice is a shotgun, right?"

"That'll do!"

We all piled into Dave's big Lexus SUV and rolled over to Beaver Creek, toward the Kmart. We were cruising through the dregs of the last century—in style and yet with an anxious knot in our stomachs.

On the way to the store, we eased the tension by catching up and talking trash.

Marcus was an artist with a thriving business making high-end T-shirts. His long locks, which had not been cut since he was a small child, profoundly proclaimed his Jamaican heritage and Rastafarian faith. Sedar, as I knew him as a child, was now Yusuf. He had gone deeper into his Islamic faith, which he proudly displayed in his traditional dress.

Dave listened attentively to the stories and drove. They asked about my flight. I told them I had been checked four times at the airport, by someone who apparently thought I was an Arab. Then I told them what happened to the cowboy. Everybody laughed.

When we walked into the Kmart, it was clear their staff didn't see us the way we saw one another. The greeter at the front door looked like a farmer's widow: plaid shirt, jeans, hair pulled back, and sun-drenched creases in her face.

When the old lady saw us, she stopped breathing for a second. "How may I help you boys?"

Ever the comedian, Dave replied in full baritone, "Ma'am, where's the gun section?"

She stopped breathing again. And then she walked sideways, the way a crab moves. Jerkily, keeping her eyes on us until she got hold of the handset for the PA system. "Help needed in the gun section. HELP needed in the gun section. H-E-L-P needed in the G-U-N section."

We took a deep breath and walked through the second set of glass doors into the store. I glanced at my brothers. The diversity that we represented within our community had always made me look forward to reunions like this. However, that night, it occurred to me that what made us beautiful to one another may have made us terrifying to her.

While we saw one another's culture, faith, courage, and genius, she seemed to see something else. A bald-headed Black man in urban dress. A Jamaican. An orthodox Muslim. A fourth guy who looked vaguely Arab. It occurred to me that she may have stopped breathing simply because she thought of us as the four horsemen of the Apocalypse.

It felt like others might feel that way too. It was as if you could hear a silent cacophony of safeties easing off weapons hidden beneath long shirts and in purses.

As we walked through the store, it felt like we had targets on our backs.

Once we made it to the gun section, a teenage boy popped out from the storage area to greet us. To me he looked like Howdy Doody: skinny, awkward, bright red hair, red freckles, and big old smile. "How may I help you, gentlemen?" he said.

Dave upped the ante again. "I want the biggest, blackest, most powerful shotgun that you have, son." Howdy Doody inhaled audibly, and then nervously rattled the keys as he attempted to open the gun cabinet. He handed Dave a child's shotgun. I knew it was going to be a long night.

I got down on my knees and started going through the shotgun shells, looking for the finest-grade bird shot they had. That way, if anybody got hit, no one got hurt too bad. And I needed a trigger lock. In time, I found both.

By then, Dave was halfway down the rack. Howdy Doody literally kept handing him gun after gun. There were thirty in the case. A crowd had gathered. Half of the people there knew he was the local comedic legend Dave Chappelle. The other half could have been the local militia. I wasn't sure.

Dave was holding court. Every time the young man handed him a gun, a real serious look crept up on Dave's face. He would drop the gun toward the floor, adjust his grip, and then snap it up a little bit before saying, "Get off my porch. Nope, still too small." He did this, gun after gun. Finally, I walked up to Howdy Doody and whispered, "Sir, respectfully, just give him the one at the end. Flat black, double barrel, extended length, Mossberg twelve-gauge. Yeah, that one, son. That'll do."

He rattled his keys again. *That* gun was in the other cabinet. Finally, he got it and handed it to Dave, who did one more routine.

"Get off my . . . Perfect. This is perfect. We'll take this one"

Marcus, Yusuf, and I looked at one another as if we were about to play the craziest game of hot potato ever attempted. No one wanted to touch that gun. Not in that store.

Two decades in the future, Johnny Crawford would be killed at the nearby Walmart while buying a red Ryder BB gun for his son. An audibly drunk woman called the police and said there was a Black man with a gun in the store. When the police officer arrived at Johnny's aisle,

Johnny was on his cell phone with his mother. The Red Ryder was still in the box and Johnny was leaning on the butt of the boxed, old-fashioned BB gun as a sort of cane. The police officer shot and killed Johnny on sight.

Crawford's killing was far in the future. On that night, we were terrified by the prospect of trying to carry a shotgun, unloaded no less, through a store full of people with concealed-carry permits and automatic pistols— all revved up by 24-hour news and local pastors predicting mayhem.

And then Howdy Doody came to our rescue.

"Gentlemen, please let me take it to the car for you. I have to. State law." He led the way to the parking lot, holding the extra-long gun like a flagpole. We filed in behind him, the four horsemen happily riding in the wake of Howdy Doody's one-man parade. We all exhaled with relief.

When we got back to the ranch, I gathered everybody for a shooting lesson. I told them all they had to do was hit the empty five-gallon water jug set on top of a four-inch-square fence post. Candidly, a breeze could knock it off. From ten paces away, the shotgun spray was wider than the bottle itself. Anywhere close and the bottle would fall off.

Dave missed. Marcus missed. Yusuf missed. I took a deep breath. I feared it was about to be a long night.

I decided to cut it short. I asked them to each step five paces closer. Now we were just fifteen feet away. I went back through how to aim, how to hold the weapon, and how to make sure that you don't dislocate your shoulder in the process. I loaded the gun before handing it to Dave. Bam! The jug fell off. I asked Dave to point the gun toward the ground. I walked over, picked up the jug, set it back on the post.

After that it was easy. Bam! Bam! Bam! Marcus hit it. Yusuf hit it. And then I took a shot for fun.

"Boys! Shooting practice is officially over. Congrats, you've all passed!"

With that, I unloaded the gun and waited for it to cool down. I stored all the ammunition at the top of the closet in the garage, where no one else would find it unless they knew it was there. I hid the gun, bagged and locked, in another closet.

Time to get back to celebrating. Time to party like it was 1999. We headed into Yellow Springs to partake in the local celebrations.

Two years later, I still had the key to the trigger lock. During my next visit to Dave's house, I asked him, "Hey, where's the gun?"

"What gun?" he responded, confused. His eyes twinkled as he remembered. "Oh, the shotgun."

"Yeah, here are the keys to the trigger lock."

"What? For two years, if I needed to use that gun, the trigger would've been locked?"

"Dave," I replied, "honestly, I was a little worried, man. Nothing to do with you. Just guns in general. When you haven't grown up around them, they can be especially dangerous."

"I get it."

"Well, I'm glad you're not too interested in it. I'm sure you'll be a fine gun owner." I handed him the keys.

As I walked away, I smiled. I knew why Dave had never looked for his gun.

First, we had both been raised by men who prized courage above all else and were brothers in every way except by color and blood. As my father once told me, "Don't fear *fear*. We are all human. We all get afraid sometimes. What matters most is what you do with that fear. Act in response to your fear often enough, and one day you will end up a coward. Act in spite of your fear often enough, and one day you'll get the chance to be a hero.

Second, when the sun had set the next day and every day after, there was no race war, no apocalyptic strife, no cataclysm of any sort.

Third, and most important, like all our parents and theirs before them, we were committed to ultimately loving our neighbors as ourselves. All of them. It's the core of the Golden Rule that unites all faiths. And for a Christian and a Muslim, like me and Dave, it all comes back to Jesus's lesson about the Jericho Road: Your neighbor is not just the person walking next to you, it is also the man in the ditch. Yes, that includes everybody—even the ones prophesizing about the Apocalypse and buying a lot more guns than we did.

It's true we all get scared. It's also true that almost all of us ultimately want the same things: a better life for our kids, a country where we can speak and worship freely (or not worship if that's our choice), safe communities, good schools—a nation worthy of its promise of liberty and justice for all.

Our ancestors may have arrived on ships, or by plane, on foot, or in another way defined by the traditions of a particular Native American tribe. Regardless, if there is one thing we have in common, it's that we are all in the same boat now. And for most of us, it's the only boat we will ever have.

2

WHO IS MY FAMILY?

H ey, Cousin Ben."

Those words, with that voice, that distinctly Southern Virginia lady accent just a shade different than my grandma's, made me pause for a moment. "Ah, Cousin Maggie! What can I do you for?"

I thought back to the day I met Maggie. We were at a "Renaissance Weekend," but not the kind with knights in shining armor and damsels in distress.

No, it was part of an ongoing series of events originally organized by Bill and Hillary Clinton and their friends. For decades, just about every holiday weekend, somewhere in America a hotel or resort was hosting a Renaissance Weekend. It was a gathering of friends, each selected because they played some important role in their community or the country. All were there to get to know one another, and share ideas and solutions for how we might move forward as a nation.

I had been invited for years, and never gone. However, this time they were having Renaissance Weekend in Monterey, California, near where I grew up and my parents still lived. The cost of going, in other words, was almost zero. So, at the last minute I decided, "What the heck? It might be fun."

Each night, I was seated at a table with folks I didn't know. The conversations were fascinating. By the last night, I was settled in and comfortable with the routine. I approached my table with a drink in hand. After a quick glance, it was clear the most interesting couple at the table was seated to my right. They appeared to be a May-December romance, but the reverse of what you might expect: she looked like she was at least a decade older than him. I leaned over to the husband, who was sitting right next to me, and said, "So, where are y'all from?"

"Los Gatos," he said.

"Nobody's from Los Gatos," I replied. "When I was a kid, those were orchards. Where y'all really from?"

"Well, I'm from Minnesota. And my wife is from Virginia."

"Where in Virginia?" I asked.

"Southern Virginia," he responded.

"Where in Southern Virginia?" I took another sip of my drink.

"Petersburg."

I almost spit out my drink. "Petersburg?"

"Yeah, Petersburg," he responded, matter-of-factly.

"Wow," I said slowly. "My family is from Petersburg. What are her family names?"

He looked at his wife and said, "Well, her maiden name is Bland."

This time, I choked on my drink before catching my breath.

"Stop," I said. "Her maiden name is Bland?" I studied his wife closely: she looked a little like my grandma.

"Yeah," he responded, more puzzled this time.

"She's from Petersburg?"

"Yeah." This time with a touch of exasperation.

"I don't know how to say this," I said finally, "I think your wife's family used to own my mama's family."

He stopped breathing. Nothing about being from Minnesota had prepared him for my comment.

He turned and whispered in his wife's ear. They switched chairs. I took a big gulp of my drink and pondered what I had just done.

She stared at me real close. She kept staring. "Come here, baby! Give me a hug!" she exclaimed. "Let me look at you. Yeah, I always knew I had Black family." I was quiet. "You see, Mammy raised me until I was twelve."

"Mammy," she continued, "had to be blood. She could get on the party line when my ma and her sisters were squabbling, and squash any fight in an instant. In the Bland family, only blood can do that."

Mammy? Just *Mammy?* I always thought Southern ladies would say *my mammy*, like a rich kid might say *my nanny*. But she was saying Mammy, like you'd say *Mommy*.

I asked her if Mammy was still around. She said, "I don't know. I haven't seen her since I was twelve. Mama sent Mammy back to Virginia. And that was the last I saw of her. I always knew we had to have more Black family than her. So tell me about my other cousins!"

We talked for the rest of the night. I told her about how my family made it to California. She told me how her family came out to San Francisco during the Great Depression, bringing a small fortune with them and seeking to build more. She was born when her mom was forty-two, an unexpected blessing. Her mother had asked for Mammy to be sent out from Virginia to raise her. Her mother needed to continue lunching and attending parties, working her way into San Francisco high society. My newfound cousin had been the odd one out: the surrogate daughter of a Black mother, a soon-to-be flower child raised in an antebellum family.

One of her earliest childhood memories was of her brothers dueling with swords because one of them dared bring Abraham Lincoln's biography into the house. The sword fight didn't end until they drew blood. I was fascinated. And yet it all left me a bit unsettled.

You see, my family is not just light-skinned; we are very light-skinned, especially the elders on the Bland side. The family lore is of rape after rape after rape. My grandma's body, you could say, is a Confederate monument. She is lighter than me. Her mother was lighter than her. And yet the knowledge of how we came to be so light-skinned never left any room for confusion about what side of the line we were on.

When she was a young adult, my mom once committed the sin of marveling about the ways we might otherwise be classified. She had just landed in the Philippines as a member of the Peace Corps. The racial caste system in the Philippines was a product of Spanish colonialism: very different from that developed by the English in the United States.

My mother sent her grandmother a letter saying, "Well, over here in the Philippines, I would be considered *this*, and Granddad would be considered *that*, and Mama would be considered *this*. And you would be considered *that*."

She got the shortest reply she ever received back from her grandmother: "Baby, you are 100% Negro. Never forget it. Love, Grandma." Virginia codified the One-Drop rule four decades earlier in 1924. However, the second-class of being a negro had defined my great-grandmother's entire social existence since the day she was born. To her, such worldly talk about other possibilities was triggering—it raised the specter of the betrayal that she was passing for White. Sure, she could do it. But why? Everyone else she loved would still be trapped in the hell that is being Black in Jim Crow America, and she would be trapped in the hell that is denial of one's family.[1]

( )

I imagine her grandmother writing that letter in the same cursive that I now see on my grandma's birth certificate. My great-grandmother wrote my grandmother's birth certificate herself as she did for every Negro child in her Virginia county at that time. Back then, the county clerk would explain, "We don't write birth certificates for cows, so we don't write them for Negroes." It was 1916, and my people were far from human in the eyes of the segregationist government that ran Dinwiddie County, Virginia.

When I approached my grandma, née Mamie Bland, about the

prospect of meeting our likely cousin, née Maggie Bland, my grandma shrugged. "That's okay, baby. I knew those people when I was young. I have no interest in reconnecting with them."

I explained that Maggie was different—that she was born in California and had been a hippie. I shared that she was raised for her first twelve years by a Black woman who she believed was her cousin. Maggie was eager to reconnect with more Black members of her family; in fact, she had been looking for us for her entire life.

My grandma said she'd think about it.

She said no. "I'd die happy if I never saw them again."

To say she knew them was an understatement. She was born a Black Bland in Dinwiddie County, where many of the most prominent Blacks and Whites shared that unfortunate adjective as their family name. Moreover, her great-grandfather Frederick Bland was the only slave mentioned in the will of Richard Yates "R.Y." Bland who owned Fred, his wife née Nancy Yates, and their children:

"It is my will and desire that my body servant Frederick be kept in the family where my sons may live, to wait on them, and attend to home business, gardening and so for him to make his board, if no more. He is never to work out as a field hand, nor under an overseer."

R.Y. Bland had many slaves but only one was mentioned in the will. And every word of the mention was dedicated to protecting said slave. Why? Well, when the Harvard University historian Henry Louis "Skip" Gates pored over the will and other assembled evidence, his conclusion was concise: R.Y. Bland knew Fred was his older brother and wanted to protect him.[2]

It was clear the sudden appearance of a White cousin unsettled her in ways for which she was not prepared.

Then she said yes. On some level, she wanted the healing that cousin Maggie was looking for too.

They met. It was brief. The family resemblance was clear. A loop had been connected. I thought that was it.

And then one day my phone rang. "Hey, Cousin Ben!"

"Ah . . . Cousin Maggie! What can I do you for?"

"Cousin Ben, you run a foundation, don't you?"

"Yes, I do."

"Well, I need help. Hurricane Katrina has caused a real mess and we all need to help."

Hurricane Katrina had rolled through New Orleans just two days before. The country was abuzz with concern. Everyone was trying to help however they could. Cousin Maggie continued, "I have a family from the lower Ninth Ward who are in an especially urgent situation."

I had the unfortunate task of explaining to my newfound cousin that there was nothing my foundation could do. By charter, we only funded in California, and we only funded civil rights advocacy. Direct aid to individuals in Louisiana was way out of our territory.

"Well, just listen to me," she insisted.

"All right, cousin, hit me."

"I have these two boys. They're in a nursing home up in Baton Rouge, in the hallway. They were sent there after they were rescued from their family home, in the lower Ninth Ward. The parents owned a family-run printing business. But the floodwaters came in and destroyed everything.

"The boys had to be rushed out right away. One is in an iron lung, and the other one probably should be. Now they're in this nursing home hallway up in Baton Rouge. And although the nursing home is far from the flood zone, it's been inundated with wind and rain. The mold is building up. The spores are floating in the air. If they get in those boys' lungs, they could both die in a matter of days."

As Maggie talked, I remembered that my godbrother, Dave Chappelle, had called the day before to ask me to keep my ear to the ground for any individuals who needed help. "My Imam said to give alms to any individual who asks," he said.

I didn't expect any to find me, quite honestly, in San Francisco. I hadn't really given it another thought. But now here was my cousin

Maggie Bland, descendant of the men who owned my family, descendant of the men who raped my great-great-grandmothers and their mothers, asking me for help.

I called Dave and explained that Maggie needed an air ambulance to get the boys from Louisiana to California. "Absolutely," Dave said. "Call my accountant and give her the information." I called right away. The funds were wired. The two boys in the nursing home were airlifted out to Sacramento, and given a new home. Their family was able to rebuild their lives.

Maggie was elated.

I went back to working on the issues of the day in California: low-wage workers fighting to make enough to support their families, farm workers protesting unsafe working conditions, formerly incarcerated mothers and fathers struggling to find work.

A few weeks later, Dave and I were on the phone. I was the closest thing to a lawyer in the family, and he would often call when there was a difficult situation to work through. While we were talking, he excused himself. FedEx was at the door. It reminded me that I had an unopened FedEx envelope that had arrived that morning.

I reached for it. It was from Sacramento. "Dave," I said, "where's your FedEx from?"

"It's from Sacramento," he said. "I think it's that family."

"Yeah, I've got one here too," I said.

"Let's open it." I heard the envelope rip on his side of phone before I ripped open mine. Dave slid out a photograph as I slid out mine. He was quiet. I was quiet.

"Ben, did you know the family was White?"

"Dave, I had no idea, man. Maggie said they lived in the lower Ninth Ward. I assumed they were Black."

"Yeah, me too."

It was a large photograph. We each pulled it all the way out of the envelope and turned it over to read the inscription on the back. "Thank you, Ben, God bless you, the Goldman family."

"Ben, did you know they were Jewish?"

"Dave, I didn't know they were White. It never occurred to me they might be Jewish."

"Well, the Lord definitely works in mysterious ways. Do me a favor, brother," Dave said. "Don't tell anybody about this for a while."

"Sure, Dave, why not?"

"I have no idea how to explain it at the mosque this week," he said.

I paused. Then I said, "Dave, just tell them this is exactly how America is supposed to work. Only in America could the former slaveholding side of the family call the formerly enslaved side of the family, in order to get alms from a Black Muslim to help some poor White Jews get out of the lower Ninth Ward."

3

HISTORY AS A RIDDLE

The choice was obvious.

If I was going to take any elective my freshman year, it would be Political Science 101 with Professor Charles V. Hamilton.

Professor Hamilton was a living legend: one of the policy architects of Jesse Jackson's campaigns, one of the masterminds behind David Dinkins's successful campaign for mayor of New York City, and a leading disruptive thinker in American politics ever since he co-authored *Black Power* with Stokely Carmichael. What a rare opportunity.

By the time I got to college, I had some experience in politics myself. I had volunteered as a local organizer on Jesse Jackson's 1988 presidential campaign. And I had spent one semester of high school working as a page to a congressman, Leon Panetta. I was ready to learn from another master of the craft. Just a year before, three candidates influenced by Hamilton had won breakthrough elections: Dinkins, New York City's first Black mayor; Harold Washington, Chicago's first Black mayor; and Doug Wilder, Virginia's first Black governor.

For most of the semester in Professor Hamilton's class, I was uncharacteristically silent. He told stories about the Student Nonviolent Coordinating Committee and its tensions with the Black Panther movement.

He talked about modern presidential, mayoral, and gubernatorial politics. He intimidated me.

However, on the last day of the semester he issued an invitation I couldn't refuse. "Ask me any question. Nothing's too dumb, nothing's too small. It's our last class together, so make use of it."

I raised my hand.

"Yes, Mr. Jealous, a question?"

"Yes, sir," I responded. "I signed up for political science, and all semester I've heard plenty that's political, but I haven't heard much science. Where's the science, sir, in political science?"

He laughed. "Well, Mr. Jealous, I can tell you this: politics has a lot in common with physics. For every action there's an equal and opposite reaction. And something in motion tends to return to its original state. Race relations are always in motion, for example, Mr. Jealous. But as Americans, *we almost always misremember the original state.*"

He continued, "As Americans, we tend to only remember things that we've seen on a screen." He referenced the television miniseries *Roots.* Today, it would be movies like *Django* or *12 Years A Slave.* "Shows like that invariably show you slavery near its end. The end is not the original state, Mr. Jealous. No, as we read in Howard Zinn's *People's History of the United States,* before there were slave rebellions, there were colonial rebellions. Irish indentured servants and African slaves rebelled together. Figure out more about that, and why it's important, and you'll have a better sense of where we're headed."

I had a lot to figure out.

Professor Hamilton's cryptic message got me thinking about my own life. My grandma used to say the same thing: "Always remember, the first American rebellions weren't slave rebellions, they were colonial rebellions."

I just figured she was talking about mobs of angry White people in Jamestown or maybe something like Paul Revere's etching of the Boston

Massacre. Revere portrayed everyone killed that day as White. He omitted the first person killed in the Massacre: Crispus Attucks, a man of African and Native American descent. I'd always just shrug when she said that.

As child, I soaked up my grandmother's stories like cornbread soaks up butter mixed with maple syrup.

My grandmother, like every woman we knew of before her in her bloodline, was the family griot. She was the one who told stories over and over—while she cooked, while we ate, while we played cards, while we sat on the beach. She was a veteran statewide leader in the War on Poverty and a local soldier in the civil rights movement.

Usually, she told her tales, and those of her parents and grandparents, as a form of instruction. Like an old general, she didn't expect you to fight in the same ways as she had or they had. Her faith, however, was that if you knew how she fought her battles, then you would find yourself better prepared in a future fight.

Sometimes, however, her statements were riddles she hoped you would be inspired to solve, like the one about the colonial rebellions. Other times, she made claims that were ridiculous on their face, and then confounded you with her insistence they not be contradicted.

"Never forget our people were always free!" she'd offer as a diversion from the subject at hand. She often seemed to insert it as an offhand closer to a conversation about some sensitive aspect of our family's history in slavery about which she didn't want to hear more discussion.

When I was a kid it made my brain hurt. It just didn't make any sense.

When I was a teenager, I decided to challenge her head on: "What are you talking about, Mimi? Three of your grandparents were born into slavery. The fourth was a White man your own sister says raped one of your grandmothers! Who was free? The rapist?"

She just stared at me like she pitied me. She would never say a curse word. But by the look on her face, I'd say she thought me either an idiot or an asshole.

Ultimately, I relented. Challenging it seemed as cruel and futile as an atheist trying to convince a devout nun that Mary wasn't a virgin.

Historically, the women in many families and the griots in the West African tradition don't just hand down important stories. They hand down traditions, religion, recipes for success, and the peculiar convictions and articles of faith that make a family a family and tribe a tribe.

This, I reasoned, must just be one of the latter two.

However, Charles Hamilton, echoing her assertion about rebellions, made me wonder if I hadn't gotten a little too comfortable shrugging off some things my grandma said. The last part he added, the bit about Irish indentured servants and enslaved Africans, made me want to read more about the history of the South.

4

DISCOVERING THE ROOTS OF RACE

W e better get out of here. I might have just insulted a mafioso's mother."

With that, I grabbed my girlfriend's hand, and we ran to catch a taxi.

A cab wasn't hard to find in Little Italy in June 1991. SoHo—the neighborhood south of Houston and north of Canal Streets in Manhattan—was full of them on Saturday night. I opened the door. She hopped in and moved across the seat. I jumped in after her but not before I looked over my shoulder. Nobody was chasing me. Thank God. "Uptown," I told the driver. "One hundred fourteenth and Broadway."

( )

What a day. It started out as a well-planned outing in the city. My high school girlfriend, Adama, was visiting from Harvard where she was a student. I had loved Adama since the ninth grade. She had refused to date me until I was taller than her. That was a problem for 1986 me. Back then, I was five feet one and the shortest person in high school. I was even shorter than a Japanese-American girl in my class. She's still five feet two. I'm now six feet four.

The summer before our junior year of high school, I hit a growth spurt and finally bested Adama by a inch. We started dating, but our relationship soured during senior year. When we started freshman year of college, we were both in Ivy League schools on the East coast, far from home and missing each other. We decided to get back together.

I was eager to show her the city. We woke up early and headed out for a morning of shopping on 125th Street and farther uptown. After that, I figured we'd grab lunch at an old soul-food diner. Finally, we'd head downtown to spend the evening at the summer festival in Little Italy.

As we were crossing St. Nicholas Avenue, I heard a man whistle. I looked over my shoulder. It wasn't a catcall. It was Stevie Wonder's song "Jungle Fever." I rolled my eyes and shook my head. Even in Harlem, the contrast in complexions between me and Adama could confuse people. She was dark brown. I was not. I smirked. "What an idiot," I grumbled.

A couple blocks later, we approached Speaker's Corner. A high-yellow Hebrew Israelite was screaming into a video camera. I recognized him from public access television. He clearly fashioned himself as a cross between Elijah Muhammad and Malcolm X. Truthfully, he was a far cry from any of the speakers who had made that corner famous. He was nothing like Malcolm, nor Adam Clayton Powell, nor even his fellow nationalist Marcus Garvey.

What he was, however, was angry. Specifically, he was angry about me. He was preaching about "jungle fever." This was the inaugural weekend of Spike Lee's movie by the same name. It was about the travails of a fictional Black man and Italian American woman who were dating in New York. The speaker shouting at us on the street was arguing that Italian American men were frequently pursuing Black women. When I approached, he was on a tirade about Robert De Niro's pattern of dating sisters. He apparently thought that I, like De Niro, was part of "the problem."

"Case in point, another one of them up here to steal one of our fine AFRICAN queens!"

I stopped and stared at him. I agreed that Adama was a queen. I resented his accusations about me.

He shot me a look that suggested he wanted to take this fight beyond words.

He was five feet two and all of 110 pounds. I still carried all of the muscle from three sports in high school and my time as a member of a Division I rowing team. I knew I could dispatch him in seconds.

I stepped toward him with a face that suggested I intended to do just that. He took a half-step back and preened for the camera. "Oh, I'm sorry, I mean this leprous Black man."

That was it. I was done. I started to lift my hand to swing. Adama grabbed my wrist. She leaned in. "You will not be the first Black man to start a race riot in Harlem."

I paused. "Look. Over. His. Shoulder," she whispered insistently. Six guys stood behind him. All of them could have been understudies for the lead character in *The Green Mile*. Each was a solid two to four inches taller than me. All had muscle that suggested they lifted weights every day of their lives. Each of them had two hands resting on a thick faux-African cane. Each cane looked as if it had been cut from the longest baseball bat you'd ever seen.

Adama's logic was compelling. I pulled her closer, smiled at him, and walked off.

The rest of the day was perfect. We hit Mart 125 and its booths full of African scents, cloths, and statues. We strolled up to Liberation Books and spent more money on rare volumes than we really could afford. Then we took the down-home journey that was thirty-five minutes in the diner/mini culinary mecca called Pan Pan. We ended the day at a picturesque street festival in Little Italy. It looked like something you might see in *The Godfather*. We shared a cannoli. It was perfect.

Along the way I forgot that several hours earlier I had almost come to blows with a misguided zealot who mistook us for an interracial couple.

Then night came.

As dusk fell on the celebration in Little Italy, I was confronted by an old woman. She was just as swarthy as me, her hair just as dark and curly as mine. She was at least fifty years older than me, maybe sixty. She was also screaming at me in Italian. I don't speak Italian. I had no idea what she was saying.

She began waving her finger in my face. As I stared at it, I realized there was one word I did understand: *Negrita*.

"Negrita . . . negrita . . . NEGRITA!" She kept repeating it. She said it with a sneer. The word wasn't Italian at all. It was Spanish. I knew it well. And when someone yelled it anywhere in the five boroughs of New York City, it always meant the same thing: "Little. Black. Bitch!"

As best as I could tell, she thought I was Italian too. And on this, the inaugural weekend of Spike Lee's latest provocative-and-much-needed look at American life, her question was more than obvious: "Why would YOU bring that *negrita* here?!"

My mind flashed back to the morning, then further back to the troubles my parents had encountered as an interracial couple in the 1960s and '70s, and then all the way back to the centuries of African occupation and conquests of Sicily that explained why this woman looked like she could be in my family and also why she thought I was part of her tribe.

"Because I am BLACK!" I said with all the bluntness of an aspiring New Yorker. "Just like HER. And. Just. Like. YOU," I whispered intently over her finger still in my face.

I immediately regretted my comments. First, I was ashamed I had spoken so coarsely to an old lady under any circumstances. And in the racial cauldron that was New York City in the late '80s and early '90s, I knew that trying to talk it all through on a Saturday night when half the crowd had been drinking was a bad idea. That reminded me: brothers had been killed for less. I grabbed Adama and ran for the taxi.

❲ ❳

The tension stirred by my assumed-to-be interracial relationship with Adama had me puzzled.

What the hell was Professor Hamilton talking about? *Race relations are always in motion and something in motion always returns to its original state.* For couples like my parents, what exactly was the original state? Insert scene of a lynching? Who the hell wants to revert to that?

My parents' story was hard enough. They met in West Baltimore in the 1960s, two idealistic educators determined to save the world. They fell in love when interracial marriage was illegal in Maryland. They fled the state in order to get married. We built a life in Northern California, far from my mom's family and support system in West Baltimore. My father, who is White and from an old New England family, was disinherited by his grandfather for marrying my mom. In our family, the wounds from those years may have healed, but the scars were always visible, serving as a reminder of what my parents' love cost them, and us.

They weren't alone in paying that price. Around the same time, a couple in Virginia—Mildred Loving, a Black woman, and Richard Loving, a White man—were sentenced to one year in prison for their marriage. They had challenged the statute (Virginia's Racial Integrity Act of 1924) all the way to the Supreme Court, where it was unanimously struck down in 1967.[1]

That ruling effectively legalized marriage across races across the United States. The decision was one of many by the Warren Court that recognized that there was "no legitimate overriding purpose" of statutes such as the Virginia Racial Integrity Act other than "invidious racial discrimination."[2]

The Warren Court understood what my parents, my mother's parents, and my father's mother and brothers who stood by him knew to be true: love is love. That period in the late 1960s offered glimmers of hope that we might heal our nation's racial wounds.

But I wasn't living in Baltimore in 1966. No, New York City in 1991 was arguably worse. Five years earlier, a group of young White men, from a predominantly Italian American neighborhood, chased a young Black man onto the Belt Parkway because they believed he was seeking to court an Italian American woman. At the end of the twentieth century, the penalty for cross-racial romance was still often death. Professor Hamilton had to know all that. Why was he so sure in his conviction that when it came to race relations both the earliest days of America and the future of our nation would be better than we thought?

( )

The next academic year, I learned the answer. I elected to take History of the South with Professor Barbara Fields. She was a MacArthur "Genius" grant winner who spent her career documenting the rise of race as we know it in America. Her conclusion was startling to most Americans: modern definitions of race in the United States were not created until more than a century after the first enslaved people arrived in Jamestown, Virginia, in 1619.[3] In other words, "race" as we know it was not a factor for the first century of the American Experiment.

What was her evidence? In the 1600s and early 1700s, the slave rolls recorded Africans by nationality—as slaves had been recorded by Europeans and Arabs for millennia. Then, for reasons we will discuss in another chapter, traders began recording captured Africans simply as "negros." They were recorded like farm animals and other chattel.[4]

Among the many books Professor Fields assigned was A. Leon Higginbotham's *In the Matter of Color*. Higginbotham was one of Thurgood Marshall's lieutenants in the civil rights movement, and he had gone on to serve as one of our nation's earliest Black federal judges. Along the way, he had documented the racial laws of the American colonies. He also documented the penalties for transgressing them, all the way back to the beginning of the Virginia Colony.

Higginbotham's book taught that at the beginning of the Virginia Colony, the penalty for interracial premarital sex was likely the same as for intra-racial premarital sex.[5]

"Wait," I thought. "The penalty for premarital sex between an African slave and a White servant in the earliest days of the Virginia Colony was the same? Are you kidding me?"

All of those lynchings up to and including the brother run into the highway, and *this* was our original state?

Then I remembered something my grandma said one time when I pushed back on her assertion that our people were always free: "Well, your grandfather descends from colored people who were always free." I'll never forget that. Maybe this was what she was talking about.

In the earliest days of the Virginia Colony, the child's status was not determined by race. Race as we know it did not even exist.

No, in the earliest days of the Virginia Colony, the child's status was determined by the status of the mother. In other words, by the middle of the seventeenth century in Virginia and Maryland, there were a bunch of brown, curly-haired babies running free, each of them the child of a White woman who had clearly had a baby with an African man. This is how President Barack Obama descends from an African slave on his White mother's side.[6]

And as far as the law was concerned, in the earliest days of the American experiment apparently no one really cared. As for the lynch mobs—not to mention the police officers, sheriffs, and vigilantes that would terrorize interracial couples for centuries—they were still in the future. Maybe Professor Hamilton was on to something. Maybe my parents' marriage wasn't so much an evolution as it was going back to the future. The thought made me eager to learn more of the history of our nation that they don't teach us in grade school. They say a people who don't know their history are bound to repeat it. I was beginning to get the sense that learning more about our nation's hidden history was the secret to unleashing its greatness.

5

MAKING IT TO TWENTY-ONE

I remember the first time I realized history could move two ways at once.

I was in college. It was a friend's twenty-first birthday party. I was not twenty-one myself.

A toast went up to my friend for turning twenty-one. Another friend started to make a toast. Before his glass reached the height of his shoulder, he began tipping it. He poured libations of memory for all our friends who had been shot and killed or sent to prison before we got to college.

We all joined in. The alcohol splashed on the floor like rain—silent tears poured forth from quiet grief-stricken souls. I thought of many of my childhood friends in the tourist's paradise of Monterey County, California: Ronaldo, Latino, white with fear and hiding from his fellow Crips the last time I saw him; Jay, Black, who had been put in jail for stealing a pair of sunglasses from Goodwill; and Bobby, Filipino, who'd been shot in what folks were saying was a drug deal gone bad earlier that summer. Then there were all the stories from Baltimore . . . splash, splash, splaaaash.

Trying to turn the mood around, another friend threw his glass up and toasted the fact that one more of us—one more young Black man or young Brown man in America—had survived to the age of twenty-one.

The motion cut me like a knife. The notion that anyone could

reasonably think it an accomplishment for a member of any group—
let alone our own group—in this, the world's wealthiest democracy, to
merely breathe past their twenty-first birthday . . . sent me reeling.

Ultimately, I did what I'm still blessed to do. I traveled to my grandma's house, laid my burden down on her table, and asked for answers.

My grandma, Mamie Todd Bland, is 105 years old. She's the grand-
daughter of enslaved people. Her grandfather was born into slavery and
died having served in the Virginia legislature. He helped found Virginia
State University and expand Virginia Tech. She knew her grandfather
like I know her.

My grandma is the griot of our family. She carries with her two hundred years of American history, handed down by her enslaved grandparents and great-grandparents, and the century that she has witnessed
firsthand.

To visit my grandma, I took the twenty-five-dollar casino bus to
Atlantic City. They gave you twenty dollars' worth of quarters for the
slot machines when you arrived. My mother's father picked me up there,
and I gave him the two rolls of quarters, which he tucked away in the
glove compartment. Grandpa liked to gamble. It was always casual,
low stakes, and my grandma kept him on a strict budget. Those eighty
quarters were a treat. His philosophy was simple and delivered with a
chuckle: "Just show up knowing how much you're willing to lose and
enjoy the ride. If you find yourself way up, walk away!"

My grandparents lived in West Cape May, New Jersey, by way of West
Baltimore. My mother's family followed the Up South Black migration
patterns of the nineteenth and early twentieth centuries. The first wave
that we know of left our family's historical hometown of Petersburg,
Virginia, for Liberia. The next were runaways near the end of slavery, at
least one of whom ran all the way to Canada, only to return after the Civil
War to her old plantation. Others faded into Whiteness after the war.
Others came close. One set of cousins established a restaurant in New-
ark that served only White patrons. Another cousin went to Harvard

Law. Others went north to places like Baltimore and Harlem to find work in the early years of the Depression.

In 1940, my grandma took the train north from the family home in Southern Virginia. It was the house in which my grandfather's great-grandfather had freed his wife and children after purchasing them out of slavery. It was where my mother was born. My grandfather had gone ahead months earlier to take a job on the B&O railroad as a "fourth cook"—a dishwasher.[1] Even though he was a college graduate with a math degree, the railroad afforded good work, a union job, in tough times. The job cost him his mustache, a wound to his pride that he never forgot. In my grandfather's experience, Black men on the B&O were called by their first names and "boy." "Boys" didn't get to have mustaches. Only "men" could wear facial hair. And on the ol' Jim Crow B&O, only Whites were allowed to be men.

My grandparents settled in West Baltimore. Historically, the city was the South's northernmost center of opportunity for Black folks. The Westside had been home to the largest Southern community of free Black people before the start of the Civil War. That war was over, but the patterns remained. The west side had been defined by Black people fleeing from North Carolina, Virginia, and the more rural parts of Maryland. Even more than being my grandparents' and mother's new home, it was full of the smells, sounds, rhythms, and bloodlines of the one they had just left. It was an oasis for our family during segregation, just as it had been for freedmen during slavery.

Like any oasis, in hindsight its existence had always been more fragile than most sensed at the time. My parents left West Baltimore in 1966, just as the area started its painful economic decline. My grandparents, on the other hand, stayed. Pennsylvania Avenue burned in 1968; the Royal Theater closed in 1971; the old Black downtown, increasingly abandoned, deteriorated before it was gutted and then razed.

Nevertheless, my family still attended "the Historic St. James Episcopal Church," even as the row houses around it were boarded up.

Lafayette Square Park, across the street, filled with trash that was rarely collected and addicts who appeared incapable of caring for themselves.

I was baptized there in 1973. My grandparents held bigger and bigger gatherings on Longwood Street, and later in the leafy-green inner-city haven of Ashburton, even as the safe spaces in West Baltimore grew smaller and smaller.

Heroin was surging and bullets were flying just blocks away.

Still, for me, the house in Ashburton was like heaven. My grandparents' love and pride in the life they managed to build radiated. They made the house sparkle. My grandad's mother baked fresh rolls every day, in between sewing and crocheting. On Saturdays, Grandma made spoonbread and fried apples. On Sundays, she served pancakes in an ancient-looking warmer. Some days, my cousins and I caught butterflies in the backyard. There was always a party at the house, in the city, or out at a summer house in Highland Beach, the incredibly tight-knit Black community on the Chesapeake where Frederick Douglass once had his summer home. Family was everywhere.

Eventually, my grandparents retired to their summer cottage in West Cape May, New Jersey, a historically Black town less than an hour south of Atlantic City.

Cape May and West Cape May sit at the southernmost tip of the state. Cape May, dating back to the late seventeenth century, is widely recognized as the country's first vacation resort town. The racial history is important. The towns were stops on the Underground Railroad. Freedom seekers on the Railroad crossed the Delaware Bay and headed for New Jersey, guided by the Cape May Lighthouse. Harriet Tubman herself maintained a strong presence in what it is now West Cape May and used the town as her headquarters throughout the 1850s.

West Cape May isn't on the beach. The White town, Cape May, is on the beach. West Cape May is separated from the beach by an old cattle pasture. But since West Cape May is less than three hours from both Baltimore and Philly, and was one of the few areas near the water open to Black people, the town long attracted a vibrant summer community of teachers, civil servants, and other middle-class Black professionals. Last time I checked, a century-old newspaper advertisement marketing West Cape May to Black professionals from DC to NYC was still framed and displayed way up the stairs on a wall inside the local lighthouse.

In the 1950s, my grandparents rented a cabin in Beachwood Park, along the Magothy River, at a now legendary (and long gone) historically Black vacation camp in Pasadena, Maryland. It was the short-lived working-class cousin to the storied Highland Beach—a summer home not just for Frederick Douglass but also Booker T. Washington, Langston Hughes, and W. E. B. Du Bois. We loved to visit Highland Beach for parties. We could never afford to buy there.

My grandparents bought an old farmhouse in West Cape May in the 1970s. Even twenty years later, in 1993, the town remained as segregated and safe as it was when I was a kid. It was as free of worry and full of friends as the *old* West Baltimore had been for them. It was a rare refuge both far from where they were born yet still deeply connected in ways that made it feel like home every day. (My grandma once mentioned in passing that a neighbor she barely knew had lived within a few miles of her across her entire life, from Dinwiddie County to Virginia State University to West Baltimore to West Cape May.)

As government workers, my grandma always insisted they watch their pennies. My grandfather agreed.

Through discipline and hard work, my grandma ensured they rose in status and comfort. She worked for Planned Parenthood in the early 1940s when its most controversial crusade was birth control (and abortion was illegal). There, in the shadow of the Catholic Church that defined Old Baltimore and Old Maryland, and amid the Great Migration that was redefining them both, she taught women to do as she had done: have no more babies than they could afford and still prosper. For my grandparents, that number was one: my mother.

The other part of their strategy was simple: live on his salary and bank hers. That empowered two things. First, it affirmed my grandfather's role as the provider. Second, it allowed my grandma to eventually buy summer homes, land, and cars, even a Cadillac, with cash.

My grandfather loved telling the Cadillac story. "That White salesman. He talked to me. Only to me. He thought he knew who his customer was. So, I let him talk. Then I said, 'Baby, you like it?' and your grandmother said 'Yes.' So, I looked at him and said, 'How much?' He told us. I said, 'Okay, talk to my wife. She will give you the check.' He looks at us. Her. Then me. Then her. Then me. Then he about fainted." Every time my grandfather told that story, he would smile, take a sip of whiskey, and laugh quietly.

Grandma bought the farmhouse because it was tall and she thought my sister Lara and I would love to see the lighthouse beam dance over the rooftops at night while she'd sing old jazz standards and spirituals to us. She also bought it because it had two lots. She had a plan. When they retired, grandma built their retirement home on the second lot. Again, all cash. Then she rented the first house to friends. "After all," she said, "I don't want just anybody right next door."

The new house had guest rooms for my parents, my sister, and me. It had central air-conditioning and heat, and a screened-in back porch with a bar for my grandad. Every place my grandparents ever lived had a bar, yet I never saw him have more than one drink in a sitting. The bar was my grandfather's way of creating a social circle. He was an introvert who loved to listen to stories. He always felt most comfortable in his own house, at his own bar, hosting male friends. They were typically family, Kappa Alpha Psi fraternity brothers, and members of his other fraternity: fellow Black leaders in law enforcement. They included men like Baltimore's pioneering Judge Robert Watts and New York City's first Black chief of patrol, David Scott.

Grandma sold the old house in Ashburton a few years after the new house was built. After that we progressively stopped going back to Baltimore. Violence kept surging there throughout the '80s. More and more boys from the city stayed longer and longer with their grandparents in Cape May. It was safer. Sometimes we'd go back to West Baltimore to stay with my grandma's sister, see my cousins, and attend services at my old family church. Then the house next door became a crack house. We basically stayed in Cape May after that.

Back to the present. This urgent trip to seek my grandma's wisdom had caught my grandparents by surprise. However, given that I had grown up with them in the summers, it wasn't treated as any special occasion.

My grandfather was out the next morning when I came into the kitchen for breakfast. He liked to drive to pick up the paper and his lottery ticket, maybe get a cantaloupe on the way home. That was his morning ritual. My grandma's routine was always to start the day slowly at home in her housedress, white bathrobe, freshly scrubbed. There's a Southern saying that a woman never leaves the house without her face on, and Mamie Todd never left her bedroom until she was ready to present herself to the world. It was the dignity maintained by small efforts, done right, every day.

I poured myself a glass of orange juice and sat at the Formica table, with its wire-backed barbershop chairs. The kitchen and adjoining living room were decorated in crimson and cream, colors of her sorority—Delta Sigma Theta—and my grandfather's fraternity—Kappa Alpha Psi. So was the adjoining family room with its collection of photos of esteemed ancestors and picture books documenting our rise from slavery and later from the Great Depression.

The kitchen chairs were from a classic barbershop waiting area, a homage to an old family business in Petersburg. "It was the best business to have back then," my grandfather reasoned. "Everyone was looking for work . . . and a good first impression requires a fresh haircut and shined shoes!" If that last part sounded like a pitch, it was. He had shined shoes on the porch of his father's barbershop all through grade school and college.

Mamie Todd joined me with a cup of coffee and half a grapefruit, which she ate with a grapefruit spoon. I have never seen a grapefruit spoon anywhere else. My grandma had several. She is the last in a long line of proper and true ladies from Old Virginia.

For a minute, we didn't talk. My grandma could do that: sit quietly, with her posture perfect, concentrating on the task at hand. (In this case, the maneuvering of a very small serrated spoon into the tight corners of her morning fruit). She knew how to give you space to think.

Finally, I said, "Grandma, what happened? Growing up, you told us that we were supposed to be the children of the dream. We were going to be the first generation to be judged by the 'content of our character' and not the color of our skin, the kink in our hair, nor the fact our ancestors had been enslaved. You said all we had to do was keep our noses clean and work hard, and everything would be okay.

"It worked for some of us," I said. "I'm grateful to you, Grandma. But I am not sure it worked for most of us. My generation, these so-called children of the dream, well, we've come of age just in time to find ourselves the most murdered generation in the country and the most incarcerated on the planet. What happened, Grandma?"

She looked over at me. She was much smaller than me, but a giant to me in every way.

My grandma's maternal grandfather, Edward David Bland, a Black child enslaved by his White uncle, walked off the plantation at the very end of the Civil War. His wife—my grandma's maternal grandmother— had a similar experience. She stepped in the blood and over the corpses of soldiers and walked all the way to Appomattox to witness the handshake that ended the war when General Robert E. Lee surrendered to General Ulysses S. Grant. He knew that Grant was his savior. He knew that this meant his enslavement to his father's brother was over. He also knew that Lee, like many of the men whose corpses his wife had stepped over, was his cousin.

What a day. What a chance to build a life as a free man. After all, he was seventeen and the world, suddenly, was wide open.

He wasted no time. He pursued an education. He learned from his father to cobble shoes. He acquired land. He helped build a church and schools for his family and other freedmen. He reveled in watching his father, Frederick, become an itinerant preacher.

Frederick Bland relished his newfound freedom too. Finally, his little brother was no longer his keeper. Finally, he could shout to the world his faith: The Gospel that's says we are all made in God's image. The Gospel that says every man is our brother and every woman, our sister. The Gospel that says the meek shall inherit the Earth. The Gospel of Freedom.

Edward David became an itinerant preacher of Freedom too: political freedom, economic freedom. He traveled his county organizing his neighbors. First, he organized Blacks and then working-class Whites too. He worked as a teacher, shoemaker, and keeper of the Jordan Point Lighthouse. He helped lead a movement that created Virginia State University, expanded Virginia Tech, and secured the future of free public education for every child in Virginia—a legacy that endures until this very day. Along the way he amassed one of the largest Black-owned farms in his county.

The family that owned him—the family whose blood ran through his veins—took great pride in their role in founding The Commonwealth and building its plantation economy. Like his Black cousin James Bland, who wrote Virginia's state song, "Take Me Home to Ol' Virginny," Edward David was as ambitious as any of his White cousins. He seized every opportunity his newfound freedom afforded him. Unlike James, who rose to fame composing for minstrel shows, Edward David had no time for encouraging nostalgia about antebellum life. No, Edward David Bland's mission, like that of his hero Frederick Douglass, was to re-found Virginia as a place of racial unity and rebuild its economy in a way that would allow every child of every color to not just dream of success but achieve it.

Back on the farm, there was a parallel daily struggle for survival. His son, my great-grandfather Frederick Bland, was the only one of the children not sent away to college and given resources to start a business.

Instead, his assignment was to build the family farm. It proved a hard road to hoe. For much of his life, he battled on several fronts: he fought the forces of Jim Crow, disputed better-educated siblings who had other plans for the land that was his birthright as the farmer son, and lived through the deepening Great Depression, trying desperately to save the farm from going under.

In the end, his efforts were in vain. We lost the farm shortly after November 12, 1934, when he lost his life to blood poisoning. After suffering a grievous injury, Frederick decided to finish a lumber delivery instead of rushing to the Negro hospital, more than twenty country miles away. By the time he made it there, sepsis had already set in. A series of painful but ultimately insufficient amputations followed.

He passed away on my grandma's seventeenth birthday. The community rallied around her and her five siblings. The president of Virginia State University, and family in the city, made sure she could get to and through college. After all, that college would not have existed but for her grandfather's work in the legislature.

She returned home after school to serve as the only teacher in a one-room segregated public primary school for which her grandfather had donated land. She married and, after giving birth to my mom, moved to West Baltimore, where she and my grandfather, Jerome Todd, started over in his aunt's apartment before moving to a public housing project. They persevered through the end of the Depression, World War II, and segregation. They prospered afterward.

Through it all, they fought for civil rights. They built a new life in a new city that was a portal to prosperity for free Black people for more than a century. They stayed in West Baltimore and served others, even as their world collapsed all around them—just as the family farm that Edward David Bland scratched out in the post–Civil War world collapsed under the violence and crushing economic unfairness of Jim Crow.

As a social worker, and the wife of a probation officer, my grandma understood the rising tide of mass incarceration, gang wars, and murder better than most her age. She got it. She looked at me before closing her eyes and then, staring at that grapefruit spoon in her hand, she shook her head.

"Grandson, it's sad, but it's simple. We got what we fought for. But we lost what we had. We got the right to send our kids to any school we wanted to. We lost the right to assume that they would be loved and welcomed the way that I was at the one-room schoolhouse my granddad built for his children and those of other freedmen. Or the way that your mom was welcomed into the Jim Crow public elementary school down the street from the public housing development we used to call home."

My grandma was right. We got the right to serve in law enforcement like my grandfather but we lost the right to live in safe communities. We got the right to buy a house in any part of town, but at the same time, our people lost land down south at the rate of 500 to 1,000 acres per day, every day, every year, every decade from the start of World War II until the end of the Cold War.[2]

We earned the right to be free. And yet the one loophole in the Constitution that allows you to be sent back into slavery is being duly convicted under the law.[3] And, man, have we been mass-incarcerated.

In my grandmother's short summary of two hundred years of the American struggle, her admonition was pretty clear. It's not enough at any point to know simply what you are fighting for. You must also know what has already been won for you. Or you might find yourself, as many of us did in 2012, fighting to reelect the nation's first Black president while states are stealing your neighbors' voting rights.[4]

In her pauses, in the glances, and in that regal way she'd arch her back before making a point with a word, a pause, or a sigh, my grandma made an even more damning indictment. She didn't believe that my generation understood what had been won for us, the price that had been paid, nor what *we* were fighting for.

By her calculations, it meant we were likely to lose. After all, if you don't understand the true price paid for anything others have gained for you, the chance that you will lose it is pretty high. And if you don't know what you are fighting for, the chance you will win it is pretty low.

And so, when I left that day, I got back on the bus and made a decision that would come to define my life.

Grandma's historically Black vacation and retirement community was at Exit Zero on the Garden State Parkway. I was going to school in New York City. It is a long bus ride home, with lots of stops. On the ride, I reflected on what she had told me. I decided that before I got off that bus, I would figure out what I was fighting for.

I took out my notebook and started to write down all the things that really ticked me off. When I wrote something that was clearly more significant than something else I had already written, I would cross off the less-significant thing. I kept writing and crossing off and writing and crossing off and writing and crossing off.

I looked at the history of my family on both sides: the White side, going all the way back to Salem and the first European families of Massachusetts, on to the American Revolution, and through the suffragists and the civil rights movement; and the Black side, starting with the pirate woman from Madagascar, then the Black abolitionists like Peter G. Morgan, and the generations upon generations of civil rights activists who fought for and won our right to vote in the nineteenth century and then again in the twentieth century. It was pretty clear that for most generations on the White side, and for every generation on the Black side, we knew what we were fighting for.

My generation, on the other hand, had been told that fighting was optional, that we could simply reap the rewards for the freedom crops others had sown. Yet it wasn't turning out that way.

When I was fifteen minutes from the Port Authority Bus Terminal in New York City, there were six things on the page. I realized I'd better pick something. I decided that everything on the page was good enough to fight for. I closed my eyes and drew a circle. I said to myself: whatever is closest to the center of the circle, that is what I will fight for.

I opened my eyes. And there in the circle it read, "End the injustice in the justice system."

I had no earthly idea how to do that.

And then I did something that I'd seen my mom do. Well, almost. She taped up goals on her bathroom mirror. She learned from the *Oprah* show that if you wanted to achieve a big goal then you needed to think about it every day. Literally affixing your goals to something that you look at daily ensured that.

Men generally carry around more shame than women about such things. Who wants to have a conversation with your boys about something on your bathroom mirror?!

So I tore out that circle and taped it to the bottom of my underwear drawer. Every morning I would open up my underwear drawer, and there it would read, "End the injustice in the justice system." And every morning I would recommit myself to pursuing that goal.

It was easy to keep that goal central because I was living in Harlem and going to Columbia University. The contrast was incredible. White kids on campus got away with dealing drugs by the boatload, while mothers in Harlem were regularly rounded up for being addicts, and their kids sent off to foster care. By the early '90s, gun and gang violence, drug trafficking, and overdose deaths spiraled to historic levels. Harlem itself emerged as the epicenter for heroin, cocaine, and crack trafficking, and the 100:1 disparity between crack and cocaine sentencing fueled the mass incarceration of Black communities.[5]

A funny thing happens when you really commit yourself to winning a battle before you die. A little light turns on inside you. It's what we sing about in the civil rights movement, when we sing, "This little light of mine, I'm gonna let it shine."

But at first, it's not really shining for anybody to see. It's glowing just enough that it keeps you warm in the cold moments of self-doubt. It shines just bright enough to show you the next step in front of you.

6

FINDING FRIENDS IN MISSISSIPPI

I just kept putting one foot in front of the other. And the next thing I knew I was in Mississippi, waiting to greet Dave Chappelle at Jackson International Airport.

Our fathers were best friends. His father was my godfather. We had reconnected in New York City at the age of eighteen and quickly developed a bond that has lasted our entire adult lives. We both found our calling when we were fourteen years old, he in comedy clubs, me in the streets organizing. Way in the back of our minds, each of us knew that we were ultimately trying to live up to the example set by the men in our family who were the first generation to lead after slavery.

For me, that was Edward David Bland. Bland was born into slavery and died having served as a state legislator. He helped found Virginia State, and helped expand Virginia Tech. For Dave, that was Bishop William David Chappelle, his father's grandfather, the former president of Wilberforce University and the man who led Black leaders to intervene in the policies of the notoriously racist President Woodrow Wilson.

Of course, Dave had other things on his mind when he hopped into my jeep. "Hey, man, what are the cops like down here?" he asked.

"I'm sorry, brother," I started. "Did you not see the sign? Welcome to Jackson, Mississippi. What do you think cops are like in Jackson,

Mississippi? But I've got an even more pressing question for you," I added.

"What's that?"

"Why is that the first thing you're saying to me? Why is it not 'Hello' or 'Good to see you'? Why is it that the first thing you're doing is asking me about the cops?"

"Well," Dave said, "I have a dime bag of pot in my duffel."

For those too young to remember, airports were not always as secure as they are now. Back in the early '90s, it was still quite possible to travel across America with a dime bag of pot. However, once you landed in Mississippi, the stakes suddenly shot through the roof. The minimum penalty on the books for possession of enough pot to distribute was five years in the state pen.

The stakes were made higher still by the fact that the police department's intelligence unit was supposedly monitoring my every move. After all, I had come to the state to help lead protests against the governor's plan to close two of the state's three public historically Black colleges and make the third one majority-White within the next two years. The governor had made it very clear that he had no intention of accommodating the displaced HBCU students at the state's historically White universities.

Dave was in town to help us raise money for the cause. At the time, he was far from the world-renowned entertainer he is today. Indeed, the most notable review we could find was, "A very funny guy" in *YSB* magazine. *YSB*—Young Sisters and Brothers—was like *Essence* for Black kids.

The tickets were $5 for the general public, $3 for students. Still, we expected hundreds to show and the money was sorely needed. We could stretch it a long way. After all, I was only making $85 a week.

As I exited the airport, I was distracted. My hands were shaking. I had just been in jail the day before. The last thing I needed was to get caught transporting marijuana from the airport. The highway from the airport to Jackson State stretched through a particularly racist part of the county. If we got in trouble here, the common wisdom was that the officer would likely accuse us of the most heinous possible offenses.

A few miles out from the airport, I made a wrong turn. I pulled a U-turn to correct it. Suddenly Dave was yelling "FIVE-OH!" (Five-Oh was slang for "cop," a reference to the hit show *Hawaii 5-0*, about detectives in Honolulu.) I looked in my rearview mirror and could not see what he was talking about. "Dude, I don't hear any sirens. I don't see a police car. I'm not pulling over. I have been getting death threats for weeks."

Dave sighed. "Ben, take a deep breath and look more closely. It's a Crown Vic. There's a White guy and a Black guy. They're both in the front seat. They're both wearing suit jackets and they're both wearing aviators. They've got to be cops. They're waving you over. I think you better pull over."

I grudgingly agreed. I was still skeptical. After all, back during Freedom Summer 1964 it was a Black man who called the sheriff to tip him off as to where he could find the civil rights workers James Cheney, Andrew Goodman, and Michael Schwerner so they could be lynched by the Ku Klux Klan.

Mississippi's long trail of assassinations of Black civil rights organizers might seem like ancient history, but that very week, local prosecutors were preparing to try Byron De La Beckwith, thirty years too late, for the assassination of Medgar Evers. The son of an NAACP leader had recently been found hanged to death in a jail cell. The wounds were still unhealed.

I pulled into the parking lot of a Taco Bell. The Crown Victoria pulled in parallel, just ten feet away. It was unmarked. A White man in a blazer stepped out the driver's door, reached under his jacket, and pulled a nickel-plated pearl-handled .45 automatic out of a shoulder holster. He began walking toward my side of the car with his finger on the trigger.

I looked at Dave. "Dave, that's not standard police-issue. I don't see a badge. I'm getting the fuck out of here." I slammed the car into reverse. The man leveled his .45 at my head. Dave yelled "Stop!" I looked at him over his shoulder and saw the Black police officer holding up a badge and yelling the same thing.

I slammed on the brakes and threw my hands in the air. The White police officer ordered me out of the car with my hands above my head. He gave me very specific, complicated instructions about how to turn off and exit the vehicle. The Black police officer approached Dave's side of the car and did the same.

The White officer stepped close to me, pulled down his mirrored sunglasses so I could see his blue eyes and said, "Boy, haven't I seen you before?" Still holding my hands above my head, my mind started spinning, trying to figure out something to say other than "Yes, I'm the civil rights organizer you've seen on television leading the protests. I just got out of jail. Were you at the station too this morning?"

Just then, the Black officer stepped close to Dave, took off his glasses, and squinted. "Boy, didn't I see you on Def Jam last night?"

Dave nodded. The officer put his gun back in his holster. His White colleague was still staring at me with his finger on the trigger. He looked over my shoulder at his colleague.

"Billy, this boy is famous. Famous! I saw him on HBO last night," the Black officer exclaimed. The White officer looked perplexed. "Really?"

"Yeah, he's famous, Billy."

He told us to be at ease. The White officer returned his gun to its holster and asked us why we were driving erratically. I explained that I was unfamiliar with that part of the county and had gotten lost, and that I was eager to go to Jackson State because we had a fundraising concert that night. They asked us if we needed a police escort. I declined politely. We asked them if they wanted free tickets. They accepted.

( )

Of all the friends I called on to join us in Mississippi to help, Dave was the only one who responded. There was good reason to be afraid. Nine White men, including the Neshoba County sheriff, members of the Philadelphia Police Department, and the local White Knights of the Ku Klux

Klan who had been party to the conspiracy to murder Chaney, Good-man, and Schwerner. That incident and others like it mark Mississippi's terrifying past. Simply put, it's not just most Black folks who are afraid of Mississippi, it's most Americans, period.

Still, there we were, fighting a governor who was fixing to turn a Black college into a prison and do away with two other public histori-cally Black colleges in the state.

For football fans, here's a little context. The governor was preparing to take Jerry Rice's alma mater, Mississippi Valley State University, and turn it into a prison. At the same time, he was going to shut down Alcorn University, where Myrlie Evers, Medgar Evers, and the great Black quar-terback Steve McNair went to school. As for Jackson State University, Walter Payton's alma mater, the governor planned to make it majority-White within two years.

When I had first arrived, I asked Alvin Chambliss, the North Mis-sissippi Rural Legal Services lawyer who had invited me down, "What exactly is my job description?"

He looked at me and whispered, "Put the fear of God in the judge."

Then he said, "Put the fear of God in the governor."

I looked at him, perplexed.

"Why?" I asked.

"Son," he says, "this is Mississippi. Judges down here don't do the right thing because it's the right thing. They do the right thing because they're afraid of doing the wrong thing. You have got to make them afraid to do the wrong thing."

I stared at him.

"The record on this case shows it too," he explained. "We have un-earthed documents showing that the state intentionally engaged in twelve years of bad-faith negotiations with us because they were afraid riots might break out if they ruled against us. Your job is to make them fear again that riots will break out if they don't give us justice this time."

"And how exactly am I supposed to do that, sir?" I asked.

"You know those big street protests you've been organizing in New York City?" He was talking about anti-police-brutality protests I helped organize after the Rodney King verdict, the March to the UN on Columbus Day, and the long series of college protests that got me suspended from Columbia University.

"Yes, sir."

"We need you to do that down here."

"Respectfully, sir, aren't the stakes higher down here?

"Boy, I thought you were smart enough to figure out that one before you drove down here."

"Well, I guess I got a job to do."

"I suppose you do," he finished.

I went to work leading the local organizing for what would be the largest student protests in Mississippi since two students were shot and killed by the National Guard in 1970, the same year students were killed at Kent State.

Derrick Johnson, who had recently graduated from Tougaloo College, was leading the overall effort from his new home at law school in Texas. Stacey Abrams, a sophomore at Spellman, was leading our efforts in Georgia organizing solidarity among students at the Historically Black Colleges and Universities that make up the Atlanta University Center.

We had all met the summer before at a training session for Black student organizers held as part of the annual meeting of an organization of Black union activists called the A. Philip Randolph Institute. It was led by Mr. Randolph's and Bayard Rustin's protégé Norman Hill. He, the AFL-CIO civil rights director, Richard Womack, and the leader of the Coalition of Black Trade Unionists, Bill Lucy, took us all under their wings. Bill was also a leader of my grandparents' union, AFSCME.

Derrick asked Stacey and me for help. Together we formed "HBCU Watch" to expand the campaign. Our new mentors at the AFL-CIO made sure we had the resources we needed to get started. A group of

Black professionals in Jackson called Black Mississippians for Higher Education came through with the rest.

We ultimately decided we could marshal 15,000 students and supporters to fill up the square in front of the state capitol and push toward the governor's mansion.

We decided we needed at least 5 percent White participation. It was important both on general principle and so that the photos would look somewhat integrated so long as we positioned them toward the front. We wanted the message to come through that this was a Mississippi thing, not just a Black thing.

Turning a college into a prison wasn't simply against the interests of the Black community of Mississippi or the Black community of America or the civil rights movement itself. It was un-American. One thing we don't do in America, even in Mississippi, is turn a college into a prison.

That meant we were looking for 750 White liberals in Mississippi on short notice.

Now, we knew some. So we made a list. We got to seven. And then somebody remembered that there were two professors with ponytails at Millsaps College who were not on the list. Millsaps is known as the Harvard of Mississippi. It's a great private liberal arts college, but liberal arts in Mississippi doesn't mean *liberal*. Still, we put down the two professors with ponytails. That got us to nine. Someone hollered, "Ben, what about yo' daddy? Would he come?" The room laughed. I said, "Maybe. That'll be 10. Where are we gonna get the other 740?" The room got quiet.

Sitting in the corner was a guy who didn't quite think like the rest of us. He kept to himself. He was brilliant. He was also a little socially awkward. As we racked our brains for other White liberals to include on the list, he was loudly flipping through a wall calendar in front of him.

Suddenly, he exclaimed, "Ben! Ben! Ben!"

I was startled. "Yeah, man, what's up?"

"Earth Day is coming up!"

We all took a deep breath and began to smile. Back then, Earth Day in the Deep South was like Groundhog Day for White liberals. It's the day they come out of their caves of sartorial conformity. The rest of the year they lived in a world of Brooks Brothers and Talbots homogeneity. It was all cotton dresses, blue blazers, and pantsuits. By their dress, you usually couldn't tell them apart from the most conservative members of the GOP.

But on Earth Day, you can literally see the tie-dye and Birkenstocks from a mile away. And back then they'd typically gathered at the historically White universities across Mississippi.

We split up into teams and sent organizers to the historically White universities.

I was the lead organizer, which meant that I was tethered to my desk, overseeing the operation from my phone while our organizers were in the field. This was well before cell phones were safe or affordable. I sat there by my desk phone, all day.

By three o'clock, it seemed like things were going pretty well. Most of the teams had checked back in to report that the rallies were great. Our organizers were well received. They signed up lots of people. We were moving closer to our number in leaps and bounds. All thanks to the brother with the calendar in the corner.

By five o'clock, all the teams except one had returned to the office. That one team hadn't checked in by seven. They still hadn't checked in at ten. By then, I'd sent everybody else home so they could sleep.

We were worried because we had sent them up a narrow highway that's framed on either side by bogs—the very same bogs around Philadelphia, Mississippi, the same bogs in which they found the bodies of all those other Black men before they found the bodies of Cheney, Goodman, and Schwerner. If a car goes off at the right point in the right way, it just disappears, never to be found.

Go left and proceed forty miles deeper into the piney woods to find Starkville and Mississippi State University. Cue "Starkville City Jail"—a song by Johnny Cash, which tells the story about the day he was

arrested there for picking a daisy. Imagine the politics of the late 1960s.
And imagine the individual with the temerity to arrest the man, second
only to Elvis in fame and stature across the entire state of Mississippi, *for
picking a daisy. That* would make him instantly famous. And according
to Mr. Tisdale that's what had happened to a man named Dolph Bryan.

I was never quite sure if Mr. Tisdale was telling the truth about
Dolph or just tarring an old foe with a notorious Southern sin. The tim-
ing made the yarn plausible. Dolph had been sheriff as long as I had been
alive. Years later, he appeared at a local music festival to give Johnny a
symbolic pardon. The county gave Johnny's daughter Kathy a check for
$36, the amount Johnny had paid to get out of jail. I would note that no
interest was included. Regardless of who actually arrested Johnny, that
was definitely Dolph Bryan—thirty years of injustice and no interest, let
alone reparation. Which simply is to say that putting an adjective before
his name would be effectively gilding the lily. He was simply one of the
toughest SOBs with a badge you'd ever meet.

We were worried that our folks hadn't returned from Dolph Bryan's
town. At the time, there had been a rash of jailhouse hangings. To explain the deaths, the authorities had created a spurious theory called
"Sudden Incarcerated Death Syndrome," a symptom of some people
being so "freedom-loving"—coded language to describe the young
Black men found in these jails—that they would hang themselves, in a
matter of hours, once inside a jail cell, even if they'd been going to the
prom or were on their way to Harvard University.

Suffice to say, we had reason to worry. On top of that, a week earlier
the Ku Klux Klan put out a press release saying that they were going to kill
one of the leaders of our march if Byron De La Beckwith, the man on trial
for assassinating Medgar Evers, was convicted. They called most nights
to threaten me. They seemed to know that my bed was the office couch.

The threats had become so specific, we asked the police department
to tell us what we should do if someone attacked our offices with Molo-
tov cocktails and machine guns like they had the *Jackson Advocate* just

a couple of years before. Given our "office" was actually half of a duplex house with single-wall construction, they said the only safe place would be the old iron bathtub. They noted that my six-foot-four-inch frame was too big to completely fit in it. Then they added, "Don't worry, all they are probably going to do is drive by and throw a firebomb through the window. So go buy a surplus wool army blanket and keep it real close." I noted their use of the word "probably." I also soon found out just how hard it was to find a wool blanket in the summer in Mississippi.

The phone rang at around 1:00 a.m., and it occurred to me it might be the Klan again. I picked it up anyway, said hello, and heard the voice I had been waiting for. It was Felix Garth, the organizer I'd sent to Mississippi State University in Starkville.

"Ben," Felix said, "we had a problem up at State. And we don't know what to do. We need you to get down here to the Waffle House at the corner of I-55 and High Street so we can figure it out."

I was there in a matter of minutes. I ordered my double pecan waffles as I walked through the door, slid into the booth, and asked, "What happened, boys?"

"Well, Ben, we did exactly what you said. We got there early. We asked to speak at the end of the program, which they said was around two o'clock, when the crowd was at its largest. They agreed. We thought, 'This is great.' But two o'clock came and the program was still going. At two thirty, we noticed that they were breaking down the protest microphones and preparing to bring on the band, and we said, 'Wait, wait, wait, you said we could speak.' They said, "No, y'all asked to speak at 'the end.' Y'all can speak after the party that's coming up next."

Well, by that time the environmentalist gathering had turned into a frat party. No more tie-dyes. Just a lot of KA hats. (The Kappa Alpha Order is a fraternity that was founded by many of the men who started the Klan. Their biggest party every year was an "Old South" party.) After 11 p.m., and following "Free Bird" and the third encore of "Sweet Home Alabama," they invited our organizers up on the stage.

"We went up there and said, 'We need your help to save the Black colleges,'" Felix recounted. "And a whole group of drunk frat boys started chanting, 'Get a rope, get a rope, get a rope.'"

"Well, then we did a crazy little Mississippi two-step—you know, the one where you walk as fast as you possibly can and yet slow enough that your knees don't buckle, so they don't think you're running, and they don't give chase. And then we drove just as fast as we could to get out of there— but slow enough that we did not attract the attention of Sheriff Bryan's deputies. And, well, now we're here and we don't know what to do."

At that moment, it was like a cold wind hit the back of our necks. We started to look around. This particular Waffle House was located between a Black college and two White colleges. It typically had a diverse mix of students in it. But that night, we were the only Black folks in there. There wasn't even a Black dishwasher.

On top of that, there was an old guy, still fairly fit but old, with white feathered hair and gold rings on every finger. He was wearing a long white shirt hanging nine inches below his waistband. He was staring at us and not smiling. That nine inches was significant because back then in Mississippi, for a hundred dollars and no felonies, you could get a license to carry a concealed firearm.

The man walked over to us holding a set of to-go bags. Back then, they were large paper grocery sacks. He drew close. "Are you-all the boys I've been seeing on television?" he asked.

Now, I was from Northern California and West Baltimore by way of New York City. One of my guys was from Chicago. Felix was from St. Louis. The third was from New Orleans. We might say we were each other's *boys*. But we were definitely not accustomed to answering when an old White man in Mississippi called us "*boy*." Yet, given all the threats and the fact that we were the only Black folks in the restaurant, we gave the only logical response, which was, "Yes, sir."

He said, "Hold on a second." He turned around real slowly to put down his gargantuan to-go bags. Two of my organizers were football players, and they indicated with their eyes that we could no longer see his dominant hand and feared he might have a gun. The lead one, Felix Garth, gave me a look that said, "Respectfully, you're from California by way of New York City. Let us take care of him."

With my last bit of positional power, I slapped my hand on the table and said, "Fellas, let's just hear what the man has to say." Felix gave me a look back that said, "If he shoots us, and he doesn't get to you, my mom is coming for you next." He liked to brag that his mom was the daughter of a Black woman and a notorious Southern mafioso. He wasn't joking. Nor was I.

The old man turned around and we watched for his hand. Time suddenly crawled as if we were trapped in a slow-motion video. Our fear that he might be reaching for a gun continued to mount.

Then suddenly he reached out to shake our hands. "Well, I'm so proud of you boys," he smiled warmly. "Man, if I had been born a *nigger* in this crazy state, I'd be mad as hell too."

Okay, this man has called us *boy* twice. He's called us *nigger* once. And yet our hearts began to flutter, as if we had just found the most grammatically challenged ally in America. After all, this man had truly taken a moment to think about what it must be like to be Black in Mississippi when they're fixing to turn one of your colleges into a prison.

"Look," he continued, "if you need anything, if you need money, if you need somebody for that crazy march of yours, if you need a car, you come see me. I own the used-car lot right down Highway 49."

That night, we slept a little easier.

The next morning, we woke up. We did what good organizers do: we debriefed on the day before. We talked about the lessons learnt. We decided that we had made one mistake that day: we had assumed. We knew who our friends absolutely were: anybody at an Earth Day rally. We turned out to be about 90 percent right. And we had assumed we knew who our friends absolutely were not: old white men at the Waffle House staring at us and not smiling. In that case, we turned out to be 100 percent wrong.

So we decided to do two things. First, we would go find him, invite him to the march, and get his donation.

Second, from that day forward, we would talk to anybody and everybody who would listen to us as if they were a friend who we were confident would understand the righteousness of our cause. With the optimism and the conviction with which we spoke to a Black church, we would speak to a White church. We spoke to Republicans. We spoke to Democrats. This wasn't just anti-Black or anti-civil-rights or merely the ideas of a single wayward politician; this was un-American. It was even un-Mississippian.

We approached the media in the same way. That was new for us. Poverty is a powerful force for historic preservation. And in 1993 in the poorest state in the union, we had been sternly advised not to waste time trying to convince any of the White-owned media outlets of the worthiness of our cause. Black folks called the local daily, the *Clarion-Ledger*, the *Clarion-Liar*. "That's all you have to know," I was told. The ABC and CBS affiliates were no different. They all had supported segregation one way or another for at least a generation after the 1954 *Brown v. Board of Education* Supreme Court decision that outlawed it.

That just left us the NBC affiliate. It was owned by Aaron Henry, the former longtime president of the Mississippi State Conference of the NAACP. He chaired an investment group that bought it after a prolonged legal battle.

When we reached out, we discovered that many of the reporters from out of town were sympathetic. Their coverage quickly began to favor our position.

We won the case in the court of public opinion. And then we won in court.

Those schools are still open to this day. That prison was never built. It's amazing what can happen when you extend the hand of friendship across old lines of division.

7

THE PERSONAL PERILS
OF PEACEMAKING

I arrived at the South African Consulate in New York City as I had many times before, eager to see Archbishop Desmond Tutu.

The archbishop had been my hero ever since I was a young teenager. I saw him on the nightly news, the most renowned, free-moving leader of the anti-apartheid movement when Mandela was in prison. He once famously stood before a lynch mob that had formed to kill a man accused of being an informant for the South African Defense Force, which brutally defended the apartheid regime.

Local people had accused, tried, and convicted the man in the makeshift courts that Black communities were forced to rely on in the absence of a justice system that honored their equality. The worst punishment, the maximum they could give, was death by necklacing, a particularly South African form of lynching reserved for Black South Africans who were found to have betrayed the fight for freedom.[1] Gasoline was poured into a tire to be lit ablaze and the burning tire would be dropped on the victim's head, the flames engulfing them, burning them to death in the middle of the street.

In grainy footage on the nightly news, Archbishop Tutu stepped between the crowd and the victim. He put his hands up. He calmed them. They extinguished the tire. The man was spared.[2]

The archbishop had been instrumental in the creation of the Truth and Reconciliation Commission, which he chaired. It was dedicated to healing and reconciling the country in the wake of apartheid and the horrors inflicted on generations of South Africans. Unlike the Nuremberg trials that prosecuted Nazis after their downfall, the commission had the harder job of implementing restorative justice. There were very few comparisons in world history. Archbishop Tutu's courage to embrace love over hate is widely heralded for the commission's many successes.

In my Washington, D.C., office at the National Coalition to Abolish the Death Penalty, a tribute to his courage hung on my wall. It was a painting of a dozen men stabbing each other in the back and one holding up his hands and dropping a knife. The words read simply, "'An eye for an eye makes the whole world blind.' —Desmond Tutu."

I knew today's meeting would be bittersweet. It was our last. We had worked together to keep a South African juvenile off death row in Mississippi. Accused of being an accomplice, he was far from it.

This was the first death penalty case to make the front page of *The Wall Street Journal* in more than twenty years. Anyone who looked at it objectively came to the same conclusion: the adult killer was a sociopath, and the juvenile who witnessed his violence was another victim of it, one that he had let live. In the eyes of the Mississippi prosecutor who had sought the death penalty for the sixteen-year-old South African as an accomplice while giving the American killer a plea deal, he was simply another young Black man. That's when the judge took the death penalty off the table. Because of the archbishop's intervention, the victim's family agreed to allow young Azikiwe to plead to lesser charges. He was sentenced to thirty-five years.

Still, I looked forward to seeing the archbishop. Members of my family have been Black Episcopalian priests for as long as such priests have been in America. Episcopalians and Anglicans are globally the same denomination. We all took special pride in him, but more than anything I always looked forward to his wit. His humor was exceeded only by his grace, and his wit was sharp and ruthless.

As I sat in the anteroom, I thought about our previous meeting. It was in the residence of Franklin Sonn, Nelson Mandela's first ambassador to the United States. The archbishop relayed to the ambassador his experiences in visiting Azikiwe "Azi" Kambule at a jail in Canton, Mississippi. "The place," he said, "is as bad as any place in our country. Just as racist, just as terrible." After we finished briefing the ambassador, the archbishop and I lingered and talked a bit more. I never wanted to leave his presence.

His daughter Thandi and I had become friends through the campaign. She was a student at Emory University in Georgia, and was there that night to make sure that the archbishop's grandchild saw him. I was eager to catch up with her. Together, we had driven throughout the South helping to organize other South African expats to support Azi. We raised money for his defense fund, and we organized people to attend the trial and to speak out against the injustice being done to their young countryman.

The archbishop and I were laughing, he harder than I was, as he always did. This time, his eyes were on his grandbaby. He was tossing his grandchild above his head, smiling, and making googly eyes, all the while fully engrossed in our conversation. His daughter interrupted him: "Daddy, Daddy, I forgot to tell you. Ben won the Rhodes scholarship."

All humor disappeared from the archbishop's face. He caught his grandbaby like a sack of potatoes and turned his stern gaze directly at me. "That's blood money, son. You understand that, right? We Black South Africans, we consider that to be blood money. The fortune was literally created off of our backs and our bodies and our blood." I stopped breathing. My hero, the only true superhero I ever met, had just denigrated my greatest academic achievement.

I caught my breath. I remembered that Thandi was at Emory in part because the archbishop was teaching there. He had been traveling back and forth between South Africa, where he was managing the Truth and Reconciliation Commission, and Emory. Thandi had come with him to study at the university.

The words that came next, I couldn't stop them from flowing out of my mouth. "Yes, sir. I understand. That's exactly the way we Black Americans feel about the fortunes that built places like Emory University."

The archbishop stopped breathing. I imagine he thought to himself, "I can't believe this little colored boy just called me out in front of my daughter." And then like a crack moving across the face of an eggshell when it's broken from the inside, a smile spread across his face slowly, and then suddenly he roared with laughter and said, "Yes, son, that is exactly right, son! Exactly right!"

Now, months later, I laughed quitely to myself and smiled as I remembered that conversation. Just then the door opened, and the secretary said, "The archbishop will see you now." I walked in.

He said, "Ben, sit down."

"It's good to see you, Archbishop, how are you?"

"I'm not well," he said.

"What's wrong, Archbishop?"

He said, "I made a grave mistake."

"What's that?"

"I provided for the mental health of everybody involved in the Truth and Reconciliation Commission, except for the translators," he said. "There are eleven official languages in South Africa, and any translator must speak at least five of them fluently. Every translator at the Truth and Reconciliation Commission must translate both for the victim and the victimizer. Everybody's voice flows through them. Every argument flows through them. Every contradiction flows through them. They must literally be prepared to translate the testimony of the Afrikaner torturer and the tribesmen they tortured. And the practice of trying to hold both voices, both truths, in their head at the same time is literally driving them crazy. They're falling apart one by one."

He went on to explain that given the time difference he needed to tend to that crisis before everybody in South Africa was asleep. Our meeting would be cut short.

I thanked him, both for his gracious focus on the fate of one child in Mississippi and for the honor of working with him. And as I got in the car, I thought about the time my own dad almost went crazy.

( )

That memory took me back to Monterey, California. One day there was a knock at the door. I held the door open, and couldn't move. An elderly woman stood in my doorway. Her head, her face, her neck, her arms were all singed. She had been beaten with a hot curling iron. I could smell the burnt flesh.

I yelled, "Dad!"

"I'm not here for your dad," she said. "I'm here for your mom."

I yelled, "Mom!"

"Can I come in?" she said. "I'm not safe."

"Please," I said, shutting the door. I ran through the house to find my mom in the kitchen. I said, "Mom, there's a woman in the living room waiting for you. It looks like somebody has attacked her with a curling iron." She said, "Oh, the hotline called. I'll be right there."

My mom came running with her purse and her keys. She asked the woman to follow her. Then she turned to me and said, "Tell your dad I'll be back in an hour."

I stood there stuck for a second. As she went out the door, she turned around and said, "Now you know why your father helps these men. Now, go run and tell your dad I had to leave." I knew my father had helped many men, and I knew the ones she was talking about.

My parents had arrived in California as refugees from the East coast where their marriage had literally been against the law in 1966. They had to leave Maryland to tie the knot. They got married in DC and then headed west.

Ultimately, they landed in San Diego. Dad's plan was simple. He would get his PhD in psychology while launching the first Head Start center there. Things eventually got more complex. The John Birch Society picketed the center. They said it was racist to give a head start to children who were mostly Black and Brown.

Head Start, of course, serves children of every color. The trope of portraying Black and Brown children as the sole beneficiaries of our social programs is a familiar playbook used by groups like John Birch try to shut down any effort to uplift our people. Head Start to-day serves more than a million children and their families, in both urban and rural areas in all fifty states and U.S. territories. The data on the long-term impact is powerful: participants in Head Start boast better educational outcomes and develop more quickly and effectively. Children whose families participate in Head Start experience stronger parenting.

My father finished his coursework but fell out with his faculty sponsor before he finished his dissertation. He had come out to San Diego to study under Carl Rogers, the famed founder of psychotherapy, but they had butted heads. When I asked my father what happened, he simply said, "Son, some people are like the sun. You get too close to them, and all you can see is their shadow." Since then, he had made his career providing direct services to people in need.

My parents and my sister moved to the Monterey Peninsula so that he could work with soldiers returning from Vietnam. Most of them were illiterate. They were completely unprepared for the job market, just as they had been completely unprepared to fight foreign soldiers under the triple-canopy jungle. Yet, despite not being able to read a map, they survived. The Army was paying people like my father to teach them how to read, write, and survive in the real world.

When that job ended, my father started running the local volunteer center. We were proud of him. Every year, they had a booth at the local air show. I would go out there and hand out the flyers. They had a clothes' closet if you needed clothes, a food pantry if you needed food. If you knew somebody who was shut in, they would bring you Meals on Wheels. They supported a half dozen other programs, including tutoring programs for kids.

They also supported the battered women's shelters in the county, the ones my mom volunteered with, the ones to which she spirited women away in the night.

One day, the director at a women's hotline called my father. "Fred, we have a problem. Men keep calling the hotline. Not because they're being abused, but because they are the abusers. We have a long list of them. They need help. Nobody will help them. We know if somebody would help them, we would have fewer women calling the hotline. We're not set up to help them."

My father made a few calls. She was right. Nobody would help them. He called her back. "I'll help them." He wasn't licensed to perform psychology and he wasn't interested in doing it, but he did know how twelve-step programs worked. They gave people a safe space, asking them tough questions, allowing them to share their pain, and helped them find a way out of it. It worked in part by building a new community that would reinforce positive values, not negative ones. He figured he would create a twelve-step program for domestic abusers.

It worked for a time as more and more men came in for help. They shared their stories. He'd go home. My mom would talk about the women. He'd go back. He'd listen to the men. In his mind, in his body, he absorbed all the energy: the energy of the victims, and the energy of the victimizers.

He was convinced that somebody had to stand up to those who would do harm, raise their hands, and say, "Stop. There's a better way. Let's not do this." He kept going back to the church basement. In time, the men became more candid, more trusting. They felt safer. They talked about the abuse they had suffered at the hands of their fathers. That resonated with my dad. He had been abused by his father too.

They talked about the abuse they meted out to women and children. Sometimes they confessed to abuses that were actually serious felonies, rapes that had gone unprosecuted, murders that had gone unpunished, girlfriends left in shallow graves dug by the boyfriend who had beaten them to death.

Like those translators in South Africa, my father started to become undone. It was too much to try to hold all those tragedies in his mind and his soul and his body by himself. He was the one to assure those working with the women that these men had been victims before they were victimizers. He was the one to assure the men that there was a way out for them. He was the one to assure us that we were safe even though he was meeting with men who confessed to having raped and murdered other people.

Eventually, he stopped. He tried to be the hero. He tried to be the one to stand in the gap. He tried to be the one to honor all the victims: the women who had been so ruthlessly abused, children who had been beaten by fathers and boyfriends and stepdads like he had by his dad. And the boys who had been violated and abused before they became the men who were now the abusers. But it was too much for one man, even a hero like my dad.

After a break, he started again a year later. I asked why. "I developed a curriculum and have trained a dozen men to join me in the work," he said. "The courts have agreed to support the program. If anything gets dangerous, we have backup."

Martin Luther King Jr. once observed, "Hate cannot drive out hate; only love can do that."

Tutu from afar, and my father at home, taught me what it takes to walk the path of a peacemaker. It takes profound empathy and pragmatism that love and courage produce only when we decide we must succeed. And it is unsustainable if we do not attend to the mental and emotional health of everyone in the peacemaking process.

8

MAKING THE
WOUNDED WHOLE

Want to freak out somebody's young adult child? Approach them in the grocery store and tell them their parent helped save your marriage. TMI, Aisle 12.

When I was home from Oxford, it kept happening to me. I'd be buying vegetables or canned goods or waiting in line at the grocery store, and some woman in her fifties or sixties would walk up to me and say, "Tell your dad I said 'thanks.' He saved my marriage." It happened so many times, I finally sat him down and asked him to walk me through exactly what it was that he did.

He explained to me that he had first helped men break the cycle of abuse of women and children. He launched his program in cooperation with local judges and prosecutors. It was a huge success.

It was so successful that after the first five years or so, another group of men approached my father. They were not abusive, but like many of the abusers they had been abused as children too. They suffered from many of the same problems: isolation, depression, bouts of rage, and anger. They asked my father to help them too.

The memories came back to me. This was the group he met with in the office behind our house. I recalled being thirteen years old, walking to take out the trash and suddenly hearing a man scream. He was in my father's office. It seemed intentional, likely therapeutic, but it definitely unsettled teenaged me. I decided I would start taking out the trash after my father's work was done for the day.

When word spread about the success he was having with this group of men, the American Psychological Association's local chapter tried to run him out of town for practicing psychology without a license. My dad was a former protégé of Carl Rogers, one of the founding fathers of modern psychotherapy. However, my dad had never finished his doctorate. Still, he knew exactly where that line was, and had never crossed it. In short, the APA chapter failed in its efforts to stop him. Meanwhile, he kept succeeding with the men in his group.

Eventually, many local psychologists began referring their toughest male clients to my father. They began to admit he was having more success than they were with men who were victims of childhood abuse.

One day, he had a breakthrough. He figured out that most men didn't actually need, or want, therapy. They wanted an instruction manual on how to be a better man. And so he created a new program called Breakthrough, the core of which was a simple theory: If men could learn how to be better friends with other men, they would make the breakthrough to being better husbands and fathers.

My father explained that most women have multiple people who affirm them. Their mother tells them they're beautiful, their sister tells them they're smart. Their husband tells them they're sexy. Their colleagues tell them they're great at what they do.

He went on to explain that many men fall into a pattern of love and sex addiction, which ultimately leads them to project all their needs for affirmation onto one person, their romantic partner. Ultimately, that weight is too much for anyone to bear. And when they unwittingly make their spouse literally their everything, the one person they go to for every form of affirmation, it overwhelms their spouse. It becomes too much. And at some point, naturally, the spouse starts to withdraw.

If a man withdraws from a woman, she usually still has multiple other points of affirmation in her life. But if a woman withdraws from a man, he often suddenly goes from one major source of affirmation to zero. My father's new program was open to any man, regardless of childhood history, so long as they were totally committed to learning how to be a better, happier, healthier man. The Breakthrough program was based on a peer-counseling model. Dad trained twenty men, each of whom would work with four other men. A new class of eighty men went through the program every six months.

A pattern began to emerge among the "Breakthrough guys." First, driven by their desire to be better husbands and fathers, they learned to be better friends to one another. Then the two merged together. Their sense of efficacy—that they could make a difference in the lives of the women and the children in their lives—grew.

And as they became friends to one another, their sense of empathy, not just for one another, but for those children as *children*, for those women as *women*, grew.

Isolated, angry, broken men turned into healing and loving fathers and husbands. In turn, loving husbands and fathers deepened their friendship with one another. And as both grew, their sense of efficacy in the world grew, their impatience with others' suffering grew. They wanted to know how they could help their wives more, their children more.

Many became advocates in the workplace and broader culture for women's equality. Not always in big ways, sometimes just in the small ways that add up. They displayed daily acts of courage, and daily acts of impatience with the status quo, which harms people every day.

When a father decides to open up opportunity for women like his daughter, all women benefit, sometimes in small ways. Sometimes in ways that are profound.

My dad's work continued for decades. These men cultivated not just their empathy, but also their humanity. A few came to my dad and asked, "What else can we do?" Together, they decided to take on race and racism.

When another group he founded, Whites Interrupting Racism, asked for White men to advocate for justice for Black men, more than the old activists showed up. A few conservative small business owners did too.

He'd been doing it for years. If you're transforming 160 men a year in a small community, it shouldn't be surprising that your son kept running into their wives at the grocery store. I was really proud. My dad was also kind of amazed. For a guy who had been screamed at, hit, and humiliated in front of friends by his own father, he also turned out not just to be a pretty good dad, he turned out to be a great teacher of other men.

"Dad, how'd you figure this all out so well?"

"Honestly, I learned a lot from my dad. When I was little, he taught me how to be a great father. As I got older, he became violent. I learned from that, too. I decided that I could be a good father to you if I just simply did the opposite of so many things my father had done to me."

"Dad, one last question."

"Sure, what is it?"

"When I was young, you were leading rape-awareness marches and were active in a men's pro-feminist movement. When you were twenty, you joined the Congress of Racial Equality (CORE) and became an ally to the Black civil rights movement. Why have you spent your whole life fighting racism and sexism, bigotry and misogyny?"

"I planned to do other things," he said. "And then one day it just hit me that if women could have ended sexism all by themselves, they would have done it a long time ago. And if Black folks could have ended racism all by themselves, they would have done it a long time ago too. I figured that women needed some men working alongside them to end sexism. And Black folks needed some White folks learning and working along-side them to end racism."

My dad understood that confronting and ending racism and sexism requires work from all of us. He had his finger on something important. Racism and sexism don't just show up in the interpersonal—how we treat others in the course of our own lives—but also in the structural: namely, how others are treated (or not treated) by society on account of their race or sex. Absent involvement from White people and men in the fight against racism and sexism, respectively, those societal structures will never fundamentally change.

9

A PANDEMIC IGNORED

If you want to scare your friends, check out every book on suicide in the university library.

Of course, that's not how the day started. This would be the day when I would finally meet the Oxford don who agreed to guide my master's thesis: Roger Hood. As the founder of the Oxford Centre for Criminology, Professor Hood was also one of the world's leading experts on the death penalty.

I was excited to dazzle him with my knowledge of the subject. During my undergraduate studies, I'd received an A+ on my constitutional law class thesis, which analyzed how New York State had come to abolish the death penalty. I had built a movement to keep a young South African off death row in Mississippi. I'd actually helped keep more than one juvenile off death row in that state. And I had spent a year working with Steve Hawkins, the new head of the National Coalition to Abolish the Death Penalty, helping him develop a theory for how we could end it in the United States, once and for all.

For twenty years, the movement to end the death penalty had kept failing by pursuing the same strategy again and again. The strategy had actually worked once, in 1972. That time, the death penalty was abolished for almost exactly four years before the Supreme Court reinstated it in 1976. That old strategy was simple: argue that the death penalty violated the Fourteenth Amendment's equal protection clause because it was discriminatory against Black people, as well as low-income people of all colors, and therefore was unconstitutional.

Not only had that strategy been failing for almost as long as I had been alive, but making the same failed arguments over and over again was actually making the case law worse. In a nutshell, this was happening in large part because the Supreme Court was becoming increasingly more hostile to civil rights claims. Bad federal legislation compounded the problem. We decided that the first step to rebuilding the movement would be to take our cause to state legislatures.

Steve designed the plan to go to the states and then back to the Supreme Court. A death penalty lawyer by trade, he recognized the futility of the Fourteenth Amendment strategy, and declared that we would seek to abolish the death penalty under the Eighth Amendment, prohibiting cruel and unusual punishment.

The operative word in that phrase is *and*. For a millennium, British common law prohibited cruel or unusual punishment. However, when the American colonists adapted that standard in the United States Constitution, they inserted *and* instead of *or*. Therefore, in order to prohibit a punishment in America you must meet *both* standards—it must be proven that a punishment is *both* cruel and unusual. In other words, so long as they are popular, many forms of torture that violate multiple international human rights treaties are still perfectly constitutional.[1]

Fortunately, under that standard, we were halfway there. The Supreme Court had already acknowledged that the death penalty is cruel—now we needed to make it unusual. The constitutional litmus test for "unusual" was state laws. In order to meet it, at least 26 states would need to have abolished the death penalty. Practically, that meant the leaders of the movement needed to become organizers. My job for that year had been to train them.

While abolishing the penalty in a majority of states would be a tall order, we were, mercifully, almost halfway to that goal already. To create momentum, I suggested that we start by seeking to abolish the death penalty for juveniles. Steve wholeheartedly agreed. After all, fewer states practiced it, and most Americans agreed it was something we shouldn't be doing.

In the 1990s, the United States was one of at least six nations on Earth that executed children. The other five were globally recognized human rights laggards: Iran, Nigeria, Pakistan, Saudi Arabia, and Yemen.[2]

I just knew that Professor Hood would be excited to have a young acolyte as impassioned about abolishing the death penalty as he was.

I stepped out of my graduate student apartment and bounded down Woodstock Road, eager to find All Souls College on Cattle Street. My sense of excitement carried me as if I were on wings. I tacked left across the awkward intersection where Banbury Road and Woodstock Road combine to form St. Giles Street. I bounded up onto the curb and tilted right, quickening my pace and anticipating the corner where I'd hang a left on Broad Street and be almost there.

And then I saw him, that asshole, the one I'd dreaded crossing paths with ever since I learned I'd be coming to Oxford. I didn't always think of him that way. He was one of the leaders of our rowing team during undergrad. He was always a little awkward and full of himself but that went along with the sport.

I'd actually admired him right up until my girlfriend, in tears, rushed me out of the crew formal.

The guys on the team agreed that Sandra was one of the most beautiful women on the crew team. I was proud she was my girlfriend and my date that evening. She turned over her shoulder to smile at me. Then I stepped away to use the restroom.

When I came back to the table a few moments later, she was flushed with anger. Her blond hair and light eyes spoke to her mother's WASP heritage. The force that was her anger did too. It also reminded you that her father was Armenian. Her impatience with idiots came from both sides. When she saw me approach the table, she stood up and said, "Come on, Ben, we're leaving." I knew better than to protest. I also knew that most of the guys who watched me walk out of that room wished they were leaving with her. For days, she wouldn't tell me what had happened. She was furious beyond words. She didn't even want to think about it.

Then she just blurted it out. "Ben, when you got up to go to the restroom, Dan started talking about interracial sex. And then he turned to me and said in front of everyone, 'Well, Sandra, you're the only one at the table who's ever had it. What's it like?'"

Like me, Sandra was the product of a mixed marriage. Some WASPs considered Irish Catholics to be a different race, and certainly considered Middle Eastern Orthodox Christians from the Middle East to be a different race, too, just like they did Black people. Coming face to face with the casual hate that had targeted both of our families throughout our entire lives was more than she could tolerate that night. I held her as she cried. In that moment, I resolved that I was not going back to the team. Over winter break, I called the coach and told him that I was just too busy. I never quit teams, but the notion of keeping a rhythm set by that asshole was more than I could bear.

Now, months later, he was bounding toward me on the street. He made eye contact with me and then looked away. In that moment, I remembered that he badly wanted to be a Rhodes scholar, but had not succeeded. However, he was still at Oxford on another prestigious scholarship.

His eyes met mine. "Congratulations, Ben." His tone was flat.

"Thank you, Dan," I said and smiled. The thought of him feeling one-upped brought the biggest smile to my face. But the high didn't last long. The experience of crossing paths with the guy who had humiliated my girlfriend in undergrad felt like a bad omen. Here I was, at the start of my graduate school career, on what was supposed to be my best day yet, and I had run headlong into the ghost of Christmas past.

My mental state spiraled as I tripped down Broad Street. I went back to the lowest point of the Rhodes process. My mood dropped further. All of a sudden, my mind was racing as it recalled the hardest bumps on the road there.

Racism is a lie based on a lie. The foundational lie is that human beings comprise different species. If that were the case, like the mules that are our namesake, mulattoes like me couldn't even have children. I have two. Never mind the fact that my grandma descended from a long line of mulattoes.

The next lie is that people's character and capabilities are determined by their race. That was the victory in bumping into Dan. My winning reminded him that his theories about superiority were faulty. Still, the exchange reminded me that for Black people in the ivory tower, the insanity that is racism can creep into almost any conversation with your White peers, colleagues, and elders.

For me, the hardest part of the Rhodes process was the interview. That is a common experience for folks who go through it. However, my interview was problematic in a peculiar way. Before I was named a finalist for a Rhodes scholarship, I had to answer one last question. The oldest man in the room had been silent for the first three quarters of the interview while the younger inquisitors pummeled me with their questions. This was expected: The Rhodes is a combative interview. When he sensed I was a little off balance, the old man opened his eyes and leaned in for the kill. "So, your mother's White and your father's Black."

"No, sir. My mother's Black and my father's White."

"Huh?" He groaned, as if he couldn't imagine a White man marrying a Black woman.

Then he began to stammer: "So when they ask you . . . I mean, when you have to . . . when there's a form . . . when there's a box . . . when it's required . . ." I was tempted to let him continue to squirm in the awkwardness of his question as he struggled to find his words, even as everyone knew what was coming. I didn't appreciate anything about this question. Moreover, in a combative and timed interview, the last thing you want to do is cut off the questioner. After all, you might insult them. You might also misunderstand the question. At the very least, you're only going to yield more time back to yourself and risk having to answer even more ridiculous questions. Still, despite all of that reasoning, I just couldn't take it anymore.

"Black, sir. I am Black, sir."

"Why?" he shot back.

"Well, sir, if you're familiar with the history of race in American law, you might recall that Black has always been an inclusive category and White has always been an exclusive category. To be White, in any state, generally required one hundred percent European ancestry. Up until 1989, the law in my family's ancestral home of Virginia stated that if you were one thirty-second of African descent, you were one hundred percent Black. I was born in 1973 and I'm a lot more than three percent African."

I started to take a deep breath. It appeared for an instant that his questions were over.

He suddenly opened his mouth again: "So, would you marry a White woman?"

My blood boiled.

What went through my mind was something between "Fuck you" and "Don't worry, you ugly sack of inbreeding excrement, not your daughter."

What came out was very different. I knew where he was going, and at exactly the right moment I remembered my grandmother's old advice for dealing with racists: "Just feel sorry for them, baby. For some people, just having to be themselves is punishment enough."

That was certainly the case here. I looked to my left. I looked to my right. The other questioners were mortified. All the blood had drained from their faces.

I started my answer, slowly. I knew he was trying to bait me into contradicting my parents. After all, this was a combative interview.

"Let me assure you, sir," I started, "if my parents have taught me anything, it's that you take love where you can find it. My parents dated for two weeks before they got engaged. They married two months later. That was thirty years ago. They're still together."

I could have stopped there, but it felt like a cop-out, and I was pissed, so I continued.

"If life has taught me anything, it's that you tend to find love where you work or where you go to school or where you worship. I go to a Black church. I usually work for Black organizations. And for whatever reason, I tend to hang mostly with the Black and Latino kids at school."

I could have stopped there but I was on a roll, and the blood was beginning to come back to the faces of the other interviewers.

I leaned in closer toward the interview panel, and smiled before continuing. "Wherever I've lived as a young adult, whether it be Harlem, New York, Washington, D.C., Suitland, Maryland, or Jackson, Mississippi, the only question is, do the young educated Black women outnumber the young educated Black men by two to one or six to one?"

Now I was having fun. The wheels were turning in his head. Reading the expression on his face, I could almost hear his thinking: "How could there be any subculture, let alone one as impoverished as the Black community, where educated young women so outnumbered educated young men?" And I went in for the kill.

"If you're wondering where all the young would-be-educated Black men are, I'll tell you this: in my generation, it's sad but it's simple, sir— they're either dead or they're in prison."

With that, I exhaled, and so did the other questioners. There were about forty-five seconds of silence before anyone else spoke.

Later that evening, I was named one of the finalists for my region.

As I was leaving, one of the interviewers asked to speak to me. He smiled and said, "You handled yourself well in there. I wanted you to know you were the only finalist who was chosen unanimously." I smiled and thought, "Good. That old bastard felt compelled to vote for me, too."

( )

Back in Oxford, I realized I was lost on Broad Street. I looked at my pocket map. I had passed Cattle Street two blocks ago. I turned around, went back a couple of blocks, and hung a left. I found the door to the porter's office and stepped into All Souls College. "Roger Hood, please," asked the porter.

"You must be young Mr. Jealous."

"Yes, sir."

"Mr. Hood is waiting for you. I will take you to him."

Professor Hood greeted me with warmth and gave me a tour of the college. On the walls hung the portraits of past members, including the real Laurence of Arabia and an Indian prime minister.

He told me how impressed he was with my passion for abolishing the death penalty. Then he explained that it would not be an acceptable topic because everything that could possibly be conveyed about the death penalty had already been written. It was simply up to the United States to join the rest of the civilized world.

I tried to protest but I knew he was right. There was no new argument left to make. My country was simply wrong on this one.

The strategy and machinations we were exploring at the National Coalition to Abolish the Death Penalty—using the Eighth Amendment as justification instead of the Fourteenth—were just that: tactics. The debate behind the strategy was settled. The global consensus was clear: the death penalty *was* cruel and unusual—the United States just needed to catch up.

When I left All Souls, I was dazzled by the college and impressed with Professor Hood. I was also depressed about my prospects for finding a new thesis topic that would impress him. I walked back slowly, my eyes hung low, tracing along the curb. Every time I saw a newspaper stand, I glanced mindlessly at the headlines.

What the hell was I going to write about?

I had spent years focused on the death penalty. I literally couldn't think of another burning topic in criminology that I wanted to interrogate.

I also didn't have much time. Professor Hood wanted a new thesis topic by the following week. I did not have any idea of where to start. I thought I might find one in the wild, but when and how, and would it be soon enough?

And then I saw the *International Herald Tribune* in a newspaper box outside Blackwell's Bookshop. "Black Teen Suicides Surge"—block caps, double height, a banner across the top of the paper. I stopped in my tracks, grabbed the paper, and read the article.

My mind raced with the possible thesis topics. With suicides, I knew that two key factors were decisive. The first was whether you even tried suicide, and the second was with what weapon you made that attempt. If you don't try, there will be no suicide. If you do, and if you try with aspirin, you are likely to survive. But if you try with a handgun, you will almost certainly succeed.

I figured that suicides were yet another unfortunate effect of handguns flooding our inner cities. The article was less clear. It suggested that the suicides might actually be occurring outside the cities, in the suburbs. Social scientists were digging into the question, too. I decided to join them. I made a U-turn from Blackwell's and headed to the Bodleian, Oxford's main library. I ordered every book on suicide they had. After that, I went to the sociology library and every other library on campus that would allow me check out more books, and did the same.

When I got home, I dropped all of them on my bed. There were so many books on suicide that some of them toppled onto the floor. A nosy dormmate popped his head through the doorway when he heard the crashing sound.

"Everything okay?" he inquired.

"Yeah, I'm good."

He looked at all the titles and raised an eyebrow. "Are you sure?"

I answered in my most ominous voice, "That's for me to know and you to find out." He gulped. I laughed, shut the door, sat down, and started reading.

As an undergraduate, I was a fan of Émile Durkheim. His theory of suicide, called anomie, came rushing back to me. It was a simple explanation that went something like this: a man had momentum in his life and then there was a sudden disappointment, and soon after, he was dead from suicide.

In America, the stereotype that exemplified that theory was a stockbroker jumping out the window after a sudden drop in the stock market. Until the drop, everything had gone swimmingly: the stockbroker had a big house with a swimming pool and a wonderful family. Everything was great. And then the markets dropped, and took with it all of his fortunes, even his assumptions about the reasons for his wife's affection.

I leaned back in my chair and thought about my grandfather's favorite photograph. It was the most ironic image in his house. In the photo, he is dressed to the nines for work, wearing a fine coat and a beautiful hat, with one bite out of an apple but his face showing an oddly sad smile.

"Granddad," I asked, "why do you always hang that photo?"

"Well, that photo reminds me that God is not done with me yet."

"What do you mean?"

"Well, you might recall that I was the 'executive porter' to the president of the B and O Railroad back then. He hired me because I was better at shorthand than the White man who had been working for him. So he fired his executive assistant and replaced him with me," Granddad explained. "But he called me the executive porter because you couldn't give a Black man a White man's job. On that particular day, it was toward the end of the Great Depression, I was rushing home to see your grandmother. The doorman who was my friend offered me that apple. I stopped to talk to him. If I hadn't, I wouldn't be here. The second that apple touched my hand, a body fell from the top floor right in front of the door. There had been another dip in the stock market and another trader had leapt to his death."

My eyes went back to the banner headline. Durkheim's concept of anomie may have been one of the first great sociological theories, but it didn't explain the surge in Black teen suicides. They were too young to have momentum in their life. It wasn't like Black teens were cratering and killing themselves across America because they didn't get into Harvard.

Durkheim's theory still explained a lot about suicide. It explained, for example, why Oxford and Cambridge had some of the highest teen suicide rates of any university on the planet. These two universities did not have cumulative grading. For the undergrads, virtually everything came down to one high-stakes test at the end. Pass that test, and you had it made; fail, and you were humiliated. Fewer than 15 percent failed, but if you were in that group, you were marked.

Every student at Oxford or Cambridge had momentum in their lives. Many had inherited it from centuries of wealth. For some, the prospect that they might fail an all-or-nothing exam was too much humiliation to bear.

My eyes returned to the banner headline. This wasn't the situation in America, not with Black kids.

Most of them were like my mom when she was little growing up in Jim Crow public housing projects. They were simply tilting their shoulders against a boulder that was trying to crush their dreams. They were trying to create their own momentum. A setback wouldn't be anything new and it certainly wouldn't set them off kilter, and toward suicide. For most Black kids, life, to some degree, was full of hardship and setbacks.

It had to be something else.

I started to stack up all the articles, papers, and books on Durkheim's anomie, and set them aside. Another image flashed through my brain. I recalled my neighbor from back home, the father of the only set of brothers on our block, a middle-class haven where boys played ball and made-up games like War! all day long, every weekend, every summer, every day after school. The brothers were beloved members of the group.

And then, one day, everything changed. The brothers disappeared. I asked my buddy what happened. He said their father had lost his job at the tire factory, walked down into the basement, and shot himself.

I took a deep breath and forced my mind back to the present. I kept digging. The more I read about what was going on with Black teens, the more I realized I could eliminate guns as the main driving factor for the spike.

Guns explained why the teen suicide rate was higher in the United States than in Canada, for sure. Canadian kids were generally attempting suicide at the same rate as American kids, but the Americans were dying more often. Guns were harder to obtain in Canada. Kids were trying to kill themselves with things like ropes, knives, poison, or pills, which could kill someone for sure but just as often resulted in failed suicides. In the United States, on the other hand, guns are nearly ubiquitous. But that would not explain the recent suicide surge among Black teens. Guns had been ubiquitous in America for far longer.

I continued to dig. I shifted from old understandings and theories and dug into more modern research on suicide. I stumbled across a fact that has stuck with me ever since: the biggest determinant of whether or not you will attempt suicide is social isolation.

A common test for social isolation is to ask someone this question: When you have a really bad day, how many people do you talk to about it? The less isolated you are, the more people you talk to. The more isolated you are, the fewer people you talk to.

The answer varies dramatically by sex.[3]

Ask six women, "When you've had a really bad day, like the worst day of your life to date, how many people do you talk to?" The answer to the question depends on the individual, but one answer is that, on average, it is more than one. Sometimes it's just one; sometimes it's six. Almost always, it's a couple of folks. "I talk to my mom and my sister" or "I talk to my mom, my sister, and my husband" or "I talk to my mom, my sister, my best friend, and my husband."

However, ask a man the same question: "If you've had a really bad day, brother, how many people do you talk to?"

Most men will mention only one or two, or they'll just say "nobody." When you dig further, the answer is that they talk to someone only a fraction of the time—a quarter, or no more than half. Men, if they're good connectors, may talk to one person on average. But it's usually much fewer than that.

That trend plays out over a lifetime. A woman's social network tends to expand right up until about a decade before she dies. Only when the body starts to fail do women begin to isolate. But up until that point, the net effect of always talking to more than one is that when you have a really bad day, your social network keeps expanding.

Men, on the other hand, grow progressively more isolated after their last year of formal education. The experience of being in high school, college, or graduate school forces them to make new friends. But take away the institutionalized support that fosters new friendships, and men isolate themselves. The net effect of talking to a fraction of a person, on average, every time they have a really bad day means that a man's social network trends toward zero. Multiples expanding toward infinity; fractions multiplying toward zero.

Suddenly, it was so clear. Black teen suicide was surging in the late 1980s and early '90s because Black suburbanization had surged in the late '60s and early '70s. It wasn't the kids in the inner city who were killing themselves, it was the ones who had grown up, like me, in the suburbs and the exurbs, the privileged small towns sustained by knowledge workers and parents with degrees.

Black moms like mine had worked their entire lives to give their children every privilege that they didn't enjoy growing up as she did, in the public housing projects and tenements of inner-city West Baltimore. In the process, they inadvertently denied us the one thing they took for granted in their own childhoods: the all-encompassing circle of endless family.

Every summer as a child, I boarded a TWA jet in Monterey for West

Baltimore, like a magnet to iron. Some kids would have protested, cried, stomped their feet, or refused to get on. I *always* rushed onto that plane. At the other end of that flight was a big city that was increasingly violent, but I didn't care about that. At the other end were all the cousins and friends I hadn't seen in a year. We'd play cards and run in the alley, catching up on the gossip, all summer long. And at some point, we'd all pile in the car and go up to the Jersey Shore, where it seemed like everyone in West Baltimore with a job took their families, and we'd run and laugh and play some more.

As my mom got older, I'm sure, the realities of a big family life were also a weight on her. When one is successful in a community where a lot of folks are struggling, it's easy to be in a situation where everyone is asking for help. That's a responsibility and, to some degree, a burden. But as a kid, there's no better place to be than surrounded by family. And yet in the suburbs there was nothing harder to re-create.

We had color TVs, big backyards, well-funded athletic leagues, and shiny bicycles. We even had neighborhood friends. But the experience of family, people who would listen to you no matter what, or stop by to ask for a cup of sugar or just to talk, well, that never happened.

And then it hit me: the headline read that Black teen suicides were surging. It should have read that the Black teen suicide rate was catching up with the White teen suicide rate.

At that moment, another image popped into my head.

I remember when we got the call. I was eleven or twelve years old. My cousin in New England had saved her stepbrother's life. To me, their family was the Brady Bunch.

But their house was as isolated as it could be, way out in the woods on the outskirts of a small town in Northern New England. She had found him hanging from the ceiling in the house, a belt around his neck, the last gasp of life choking out of him. She grabbed his feet and raised him up and got him down and performed CPR and saved his life. She was a hero. He was a mystery—a mystery I felt like I had just solved.

I fell asleep, wanting to cry. I woke up the next morning and had my usual breakfast, chocolate milk and a cold samosa from the deli.

Living as a vegetarian in Oxford twenty-five years ago was awkward, to say the least. The bagels tasted as if they were three days old and imported from an industrial factory, and the cream cheese was mixed with Marmite, a yeasty concoction I couldn't imagine anyone who was not from Britain appreciating. The eggs were cooked in pork grease. Indian food had saved my life. So, my usual dinner was chana and my usual breakfast, a cold English samosa, larger than a baseball and just enough to fill me up for half the day.

With that, I headed to the library and got all the articles that I wasn't able to check out the day before. I pulled the stats on suicide by geography, race, sex, and socioeconomic status, and the stats for handgun deaths, and went back and forth among them.

Finally, I pulled everything I could find on social isolation. The more I dug, the more the theory held. Other things started to become clear too. Social isolation tends to increase with privilege.

Gender privilege. Historically, women have been less socially isolated because they worked at home in a kitchen with other women in the family, or even with servants. They tended to be surrounded in neighborhoods by other women who stayed home. They were able to talk to one another throughout the day. Men were isolated in an office or a cubicle.[4]

Women who entered the workplace, however, didn't just become wealthier, they also became more isolated socially. Women who are knowledge workers have suicide rates higher than women who were homemakers.[5] And although suicide risk is highest amongst people who are poor, people who are wealthier have suicide rates that are nearly as high.[6]

Lower-income people tended to live in the inner city or small towns and trailer parks. In each of those, you were surrounded by people who'd ask you how you were. And there were neighborhood pubs. The neighborhood pub, it turned out, was the greatest suicide prevention strategy ever developed in the Western world. *Strategy* might be saying too much, but the neighborhood pub has had a hugely positive impact on loneliness and suicide risk, for sure—a fact more recently affirmed by research conducted during the COVID-19 pandemic.[7]

Think about the set of *Cheers.* Cliff, the postman who lives with his mom. Norm, the salesman who's estranged from his wife. What would their lives be like without the neighborhood pub? How lonely would they have been?

When I looked at the comparative stats for handgun deaths, something else jumped out at me. White men over fifty-five were more likely to die of suicide than Black men and boys between the ages of fifteen and thirty were likely to die of homicide.

Could that possibly be true? I looked at it again. Indeed, in the United States in the 1990s, this was the case.[8]

How was that possible? I thought about all of the anti-violence and "stop the killing" marches, the headlines, the documentaries, the news specials on the Black homicide rate. Why wasn't there similar outrage about the Black suicide rate? And for that matter, why wasn't there similar outrage about the White suicide rate?

I thought about my childhood friend Dean, who had committed suicide. I thought about my friend Bobby, who had killed himself a few years later. Suicide is literally a social virus.

If you know someone who died from suicide, the likelihood that you will die from suicide goes up astronomically. There was an epidemic of White teen suicide, and a pandemic of suicide among White older men like my father, which was mind-numbingly high.

In my journey to the library that day, I started out worried about kids like me. I ended up more worried about men like my dad.

When I explored the social forces driving the high incidence of suicide, I came up with a list that had more in common with the forces behind the murder rate in the Black community than not. Among the top driving factors: hopelessness; deindustrialization; downward economic mobility; addiction.

Misery was growing in America, and our racial wall built on falsehoods was hiding a greater truth.

10

BEYOND BLACK AND WHITE

Have you ever heard the one about the White guy who walked into a Black mental health clinic? No? I'll tell you.

The clinic was an act of necessity. For three decades, Monterey County, California, had had precisely three Black therapists. One day, they figured out that each planned to retire at around the same time.

They got together and decided they couldn't bear the thought. Before they could retire, they needed to make sure that the Black community in Monterey would always have therapists who understood the fullness of their lives and their challenges. Therapists who were committed to serving them in their own community, on their own terms.

Together, they built the Village Project, a nonprofit mental health clinic rooted in the Black community in Monterey County. It's committed to putting people's culture at the center of their therapy. If a person starts therapy at the Village Project, they might find that their pastor is invited into sessions with their family. They look at the whole person.

When the three therapists first arrived separately in Monterey County, the Black community was thriving. The oldest Black church, in Pacific Grove, was founded by retired Buffalo Soldiers in the late 1800s. During the Cold War, Fort Ord Military Base anchored the community, and there were tens of thousands of Black folks at every level of income and need.

As a Black kid growing up there, it was our Harlem, our Baltimore. The base for the churches. The place with the chitlins. The home of the wig shops. The mecca of Black salons, Black barbershops, and Black beauty.

And the only place where the police didn't seem perpetually incapable of understanding we lived there.

By the third grade, over scrutiny by police and shop owners in Pacific Grove had become palpable. They didn't see me as a kid who dreamt of being a doctor, a cop, or a priest. They saw me as a threat.

The annual readjustments after summers in Baltimore and Cape May were especially tough.

That winter, my dad said there was a new fourth- and fifth-grade computer science magnet program opening at Ord Terrace Elementary in Seaside, the county's old Jim Crow Era Black grade school. My ears perked up.

"Hey, Benji, check this out!" Dad said. "Wanna go? You like computers."

What I really liked was video games. Still, it sounded like an upgrade on many levels. "Sure, Dad!" My mind raced with fantasies of merging my summer life and my school years in Monterey. A safe place for Black kids to have fun in paradise sounded great.

"Read the whole article, Fred," Mom interjected. "The boy can't go. It's a desegregation strategy. Black and Brown kids from the neighborhood and White kids on buses. They're not going to let our curly-haired boy on the bus."

"They will if I sign him up," Dad said with a grin. His red hair, freckles, and hazel eyes closed the argument. Mom shrugged. I beamed.

The next fall, on my first day going to my new school, I was quietly nervous they wouldn't let me on the bus. The old White lady scrutinized me, and then said, "Move, boy! Take your seat!" I beamed and ran down the aisle. Apparently, she stared that way at everyone. My friends were excited to see me. No one seemed to care that there was a Black kid on the White bus.

The local kids at Ord Terrace were perplexed by me. "Take your silly sweater with those diamonds on it," a little girl I had annoyed blurted at me. I looked down and glanced at the sweater my grandma in Maine had knitted for me. I liked it. "And get back on the bus with all those stupid White kids!"

I came home urgently in need of white shoe polish.

"I need to go to the store!" I pleaded.

"Why?" Mom asked.

"I scuffed a local boy's shell toes," I explained, referring to a popular style of Adidas. "He told me that I have a day to fix them or I'm in big trouble."

Mom rolled her eyes and took me to the store.

Crisis fixed, I went back to falling in love with my new daytime home. It felt oddly like all of my life all at once. My whole life to that point had been a series of days on a bridge between two worlds. Now I enjoyed having all of it all at once every day.

Eventually, my classmates took to it and one another. We learned together. We played together. At lunchtime, we'd all run to the fence to watch bombs explode on the base. Our pop 'n' lock breakdance circle looked like the United Nations.

Mom worked at Seaside High School, down the street. After school some days, we would stop at the bike shop where her kids worked or the New Orleans–style diner for delicacies that couldn't be found anywhere else between Oakland and LA. The business district was a thriving rainbow of commerce. Every hue of humanity bartering, buying, hustling, and haggling. I loved it.

Then the base closed. The community withered. Old prized family homes became someone-else-from-somewhere-else's weekend place. Housing prices soared. Our oasis shrank. Still, a core community remained. And, well, almost every community in modern America needs more mental health support than it is getting.

While the Village Project was founded to serve Black folks, the need is clearly broader. It's ultimately committed to serving anybody in need.

( )

One day, a White guy walked in. He wasn't in a good mood. He was there out of necessity. If he'd thought he could get the help he needed any other place, he probably would not have come to the Village Project. It's hard to imagine that for this grumpy White man, a mental health center led by Black therapists in a Black community, founded ostensibly to serve Black people, was where he wanted to end up. Still, he needed help.

Because the Village Project puts culture at the center of therapy, the experience can be challenging for the uninitiated. New clients are asked about their background, their race, their ethnicity, their religion.

For the man at the center of our story, these were unexpected questions. For him, his answer was always the same. I'm *White*. I'm *just* White. I'm *just White*. I need some help. Can I get some help?

He didn't want to talk about his race. He didn't want to talk about his ethnicity. He didn't want to talk about his culture. He just wanted somebody to listen to his problems.

Mel Mason, the president of the clinic, stood in the doorway, watching the intake, increasingly frustrated. Finally, Mel said to the staff, "I'll take him." Mel has a certain dignity, a strength cultivated by his own cultural traditions, and reinforced by his discipline as a therapist and the years he spent as an activist in the Black Panther Party.

It might not seem obvious that an old Black Panther would want to help a White guy in crisis, especially one who was unwilling to think the least bit critically about his own identity. But that misses the point.

The Black Panthers were a revolutionary organization with a Black nationalist orientation. For them, the revolution was foremost, and the revolution would require people of all colors working together. The most famous leader was Huey Newton, and the best organizer was Fred Hampton.

When Fred Hampton was assassinated in Chicago, he was organizing a "Rainbow Coalition" that included Black groups, Brown groups, Latino groups, and Asian American groups, as well as White groups—including the Young Patriots, White men repelled by the propensity of the Vietnam War to eat the nation's working-class people. The Black Panther Party was ultimately founded by young people who rebelled against a society that, yes, was racist, but also against a society that was dehumanizing, that treated people as disposable and pitted people against one another.

Fred introduced the idea of the Rainbow Coalition a full decade and a half before Jesse Jackson would make it the cornerstone of his first run for president and Harold Washington would make it central to his successful run for mayor of Chicago.

Fred Hampton was trained as a young organizer in the NAACP. Fundamentally, he believed in a vision of America that united across racial lines. He saw the organizing of Black people as necessary to level them up with other communities. He did so with a sense of pride and self-determination that would empower Black communities to engage as equals with Italians, Irish, Jews, Asian Americans, Native Americans, Arab Americans, Latinos, and Whites of all sorts. (If you're wondering, "Aren't those first three groups 'White' too?" the short answer is: "No, not then." That would come later.)

The Black Panthers emerged at a time when ethnic and racial nationalism was increasingly the norm among young people. After forming several Black street organizations and gangs into a coalition, Hampton set out to broaden his reach by introducing the Rainbow Coalition. He reached out to Asian American youth activist groups like Yellow Peril, Latino groups like the Brown Berets, and groups like the Young Patriots, many of whom were Confederate-flag-carrying Whites whose families had emigrated up from the South like Black folks to work in the factories that were now closing down all around them.

This was the hardest alliance to build. Bobby Lee, another activist from the era, who like Mel got his start in the Black Panthers, explains, "I had to run with those cats (the Young Patriots), break bread with them, hang out at the pool hall. I had to lay down on their couch, in their neighborhood. Then I had to invite them into mine. That was how the Rainbow Coalition was built, real slow."

Over time, the Young Patriots and the Black Panthers developed bonds of trust, even friendship. In 1969, the Rainbow Coalition, including the Young Patriots, joined together in a remarkable press conference. At the event, William "Preacherman" Fesperman, leader of the Young Patriots, said in a heavy Southern accent, "We come from a monster, and the jaws of the monster in Chicago are grinding up the flesh and spitting out the blood of the poor and oppressed people, the Blacks in the South Side, the West Side; the Browns in the North Side; and the Reds and the Yellows; and yes, the Whites—White oppressed people."

Now, forty years after Hampton's assassination, Mel leaned up against the doorway of his office at the Village Project. He stepped forward, put his hand on the clerk's shoulder, and gently told her she should go home. She was baffled why this guy couldn't tell her anything other than he was "just White." That clerk and my mom were both very relieved that Mel had intervened. They needed to get home, and this situation was a little more than those two women were prepared to handle at the end of a long workday.

Mel welcomed his new client into his office as my mom grabbed her bag and headed out the front door. For my mom, stepping out into the streets of Seaside always felt like home, twice over, to her. Seaside was and remains the old Black mecca of Monterey County. Seaside is also part of the most diverse corners of the county, home to a rainbow of communities, including Pacific Islanders. It might seem odd for a Black girl from West Baltimore, but my mom always felt especially at home among Pacific Islanders.

Race in the American South is both overwhelming and simple. So, as much as he irked her, my mom understood where the angry White guy at the intake desk was coming from. Grandma was one hundred percent Negro, and he was one hundred percent White, what else was there to discuss?

It wasn't to say that one wasn't aware of other cultural influences. As light-skinned Black folks from Southern Virginia, we grew up with our grandparents' stories of how we descended from Pocahontas and the local Native American communities. We understood that there were Irish and English in our ancestry. We understood that not all the slaves came from the same country in West Africa.

It was that curiosity, ultimately, that encouraged us to consent to Skip Gates, the famed Harvard historian, taking our DNA. When we met, he was intrigued by the fact that I was a Black leader with roots in New England that were as old as Harvard. Skip helped us realize that they were even older.

He was also intrigued that I believed Maggie Bland was my cousin; he would verify that she was. When he got my mom's DNA, he discovered that there was a mystery to unravel. It turned out the Native American legends in our family were likely true, because Mom's X chromosome wasn't African, it was Asian.

Back at therapy in Seaside, Mel found his new client increasingly fascinating. As the man opened up, he told stories about his childhood, and Mel would challenge him. When he was frustrated, he would say something in a different language. This man, who was "just White," and bristled when asked about his ethnicity, claiming he had no idea, didn't *just* speak English. Whatever he said when he was frustrated *wasn't* English. Mel googled some of what he heard to find out, spelling out phonetically what the man had said: It was a nasty curse in Old Irish. By the next session, Mel was prepared for his new client.

"Sir, that thing you say when you're frustrated," Mel started. The man interrupted him by repeating it. "Yes, that. Please don't say that again. Do you know what that means?"

"No, I have no idea. It's just a sound that my father and my grandfather made when they were frustrated."

"So you have no idea what it means?"

"No."

"Do you have any idea of the language you're speaking?"

"No. I told you, we're just White."

Okay. "Well, first, please, this is what it means." Mel read the translation. "Please never say that to me or any other person again." The man responded, "Wow, I had no idea. Like I said, I just repeat the sounds that my grandfather and my father made. I apologize. No offense intended."

"None taken," Mel said. "Apology accepted. But that saying is Old Irish, which means that the men in your family, your father, your grandfather, ultimately hail from Ireland. You're Irish. And for the rest of the weeks we're in therapy together, your assignment is to figure out what it means to be Irish, and what that means to you."

Mel could see the man's head spinning. His entire life he had simply been White. White, White, White, Wonder Bread White.

The United States celebrates the melting pot; Canada celebrates the mosaic. Canada sees the ethnicities of a nation like a quilt; we see the very existence of our nation as a cauldron that erases everything that came before by pouring out a mix that's all the same. And yet it's not. The only thing that's the same is that Whiteness and Blackness subsume any identity we ever had before. The identities of Whiteness and Blackness are defined in large part by their opposition to each other. Worse yet, the labels of White and Black disconnect us from the cultures from which we come.

The White guy's exploration of his Irish heritage, and my mom's experience in the Philippines, reflect a yearning to understand the breadth of our true history beneath the labels Black and White. They also speak to the value of interrogating the origins of our elders' most indecipherable and oft-repeated words and phrases.

America readily accepts the erasure of the ethnic and cultural identities of Black people. Slavery denied us our culture. It ripped apart our families. It obliterated tribal formations. It imposed the very notion of Blackness. Together, those forces cut our ties to our ancestral cultures. One day we wake up and we're one hundred percent Negro. Our fellow Negros are our new tribe. Knowledge of any other tribe is officially gone.

Similarly, the racial regime of White and Black ultimately destroys White knowledge of self. The day they wake up and they're 100 percent White—just White, Wonder Bread White—the notion of any other tribe, of any other heritage, of any ancestral legacy or history, is gone for good.

From that point forward, Mel's client's healing accelerated faster week after week. For the first time in his life, he was part of a diaspora. He had a place of origin on the globe. He had a culture to explore: dances, melodies, whiskeys, lagers, food, and ballads. He had a people of which to feel a part, something bigger than his immediate family. He had traditions to relearn. Sure, he was still White. But he was also Irish. And with that came all kinds of complexity about his Whiteness. After all, the country clubs in Monterey County didn't exclude only Jews, Blacks, Italians, Chinese, and Mexicans. They also historically excluded the Irish. He'd always felt comfortable in Seaside and now he understood why: his people had been placed at the bottom too.

Fast-forward to our exploration with Skip Gates. My mom is increasingly antsy. Skip had promised to get back to us within six months, but two years have passed. His show is full of celebrities, and we begin to wonder if maybe we just weren't that interesting to him. I called Skip and leveled with him. "Skip, we've been friends for a long time, you don't need to sugar-coat it. If you're not interested, it's all right. Please just send us the DNA results."

"No, Ben, of course we're interested," he said. "The issue is we couldn't figure out which Native American tribe you're from. You have an Asian chromosome. You and two percent of Black Americans. For ninety-nine of them, that Asian chromosome means they are Native American. Not for you. We tested every known Native American mutation, and none were coming up. So we decided to do a global search and we found the answer. I'll see you in New York soon to film the show."

I arrived in New York. We started filming. After going through my European ancestry, Skip confirmed that Maggie Bland and I were indeed cousins. He showed how we both descended from Thomas Jefferson's grandmother. I stared at the photo of Thomas Jefferson on the table and thought, "He took his wife's enslaved half-sister as his concubine when she was just thirteen."

Skip continued, through the Blands and other founding families of Virginia. In our ancestry we descended from every king, French and English, all the way back to Edward I and Charlemagne's grandfather.

Then he arrived at the punch line to which he had been building. "You're the Whitest Black man we've ever tested."

"Thank you, Skip." I thought about saying to him the same thing I had said to the Rhodes scholarship judge. The laws in Virginia were clear: if you were 3 percent African, you were 100 percent Black. That's the tradition, and the reality, from which I come. Just like my mom's grandmother, I'm one hundred percent a Negro, and life has never allowed me to forget it.

Then Skip dug into my African heritage. Thanks to Rick Kittles and Gina Paige at AfricanAncestry.com, we already knew my maternal grandfather descended from the Limba people of Sierra Leone. They are rice cultivators, with all the qualities associated with any people who have mastered that especially relentless form of farming. Also respected for their prowess as philosophers, they are known to be both indefatigable and capable leaders.

The mystery I had brought Skip was my Black grandma and the women from whom she descends. He explained that the mitochondrial DNA contained in my X chromosome revealed that my female Kunta

Kinte, the first woman to arrive in America on my maternal line, was an East African pirate. She came from Madagascar on one of the seventeen slave ships that arrived in America from that island, roughly half of which would arrive in New York, and half in Virginia. All of them but one were piloted by a known European pirate.

The theory was simple. The founders of Madagascar were Polynesians. Many had been pirates, or the equivalent, since the day they had left the future Indonesia, first for the barrier islands off the coast. They rode multi-hulled boats in every direction the wind blew and currents flowed. Some went to Hawaii. Others to the Philippines, where Mom felt so at home. Some to Fiji. Others to New Zealand. And some went to Madagascar, where they then traded and intermarried with East Africans.

European pirates were in a centuries-long war with East African and Malagasy pirates. In many ways, the conflict continues to this day. During the slave trade, slavery was used as a punishment. When the Europeans won a decisive victory, they would occasionally round up villagers, put them on a slave ship, and send them to the Americas.

I came home to my daughter and told her all that I had learned. I wanted to break the news, gently, so I started slowly, "Baby, I've got good news, and I've got bad news."

"What's the bad news, Daddy?" she asked, sweetly.

"We are not Indians."

She frowned. "Not even a little bit?"

"Nope, baby. Not even a little bit."

"What about Great-grandma's stories about us descending from Pocahontas?" she queried.

"Just stories, I guess."

"Oh," she said softly. You could almost hear a heartstring break—the one that always connected her to her favorite Disney character.

"Well . . . What's the good news, Daddy?" Her tone was disappointed.

"We're pirates," I said smiling.

"Oh, Daddy, that's way cooler!" Morgan was ecstatic at the news, her imagination instantly captured.

It all clicked. My mom's love of the ocean, her surprising feeling of being at home in the Philippines, as well as her need to live next to the not-very-placid waves of the Pacific Ocean, made *a lot more* sense. I felt a sense of recognition too—the way that I experienced the Pacific as my refuge when I was a young surfer, my need to be on the water all the time. On my father's side, our DNA goes back to the lost fishermen who founded Salem, Massachusetts. On my mom's, we go back to pirates in ancient Madagascar.

Across the years, I have reflected on that revelation many times.

One day it occurred to me: I'm the griot now, maybe the first male griot ever in our family. As far back as my grandma can remember, the storytellers have always been women: her, her mother, her mother's mother, and so on. All the way back to a pirate woman captured in Madagascar, held in the belly of a ship around the Cape of Good Hope, sent across the killing field that was the Middle Passage of the Atlantic.

The captives were generally between thirteen and thirty-five; the traders and their customers wanted slaves who could bear children. I came to understand that my grandma was reflecting on that passage.

And I came to understand those two riddles she passed down to me. *The first rebellions were not slave rebellions, they were colonial rebellions.* And the more confounding *Never forget our people were always free.* In discovering my ancestry, I realized I might have stumbled upon the solution.

Whenever I challenged her on that notion, "Grandma, what are you talking about? All but one of your grandparents were born to slavery. None of them were like Grandad's family. No free Blacks for centuries," she would become crestfallen. Staring into the void of understanding between us was always uncomfortable. Then, one day, I realized she was in that void with me. After all, griots don't just hand down the stories, they also hand down customs, convictions, traditions, and articles of faith. Faith doesn't require understanding; it only requires the submission that is belief. I questioned. She believed. And thus it was as true as the hearts of the women who raised her.

Never forget our people were always free. It was a core article of faith for my grandma as it had been for hers. "Don't question, boy. Just accept," her eyes pled with me.

Looking back at Gates's mapping of our family, it hit me all of a sudden. What else would a pirate woman say to the first child in her family born into captivity? She'd say, "Baby, never forget, our people were always free." And how would she have said it? As a eulogy for a lost prize? Like the way many people say, "Our family used to own a farm." No. A pirate woman would have said it the way my grandma talks about history: as a form of instruction and a way to stoke ambition. In other words, the origin of this phrase in our family was an act of insurrection. Slavery was a system that could only be maintained if people ultimately consented to being treated like farm animals: bred, beaten, and broken. Any child who understood freedom was their people's history would undoubtedly conclude that it must also be their people's destiny. This phrase my grandma uttered in moments of frustration might just be the source of the steel in her backbone.

I stepped into the bathroom and looked at myself in the mirror. I thought of my grandmother's color. All of a sudden her lightness had two points of origin: rapists from England and pirates from Polynesia. I looked at my big head. The only kids I had ever seen with craniums this big were the Pacific Islanders on the playground in Seaside and the beaches of Hawaii. "Maybe that's it?" I raised my eyebrows, laughed, and whispered to myself, "Who knows?"

My mind was spinning.

Details about African ancestry had always remained captured in a haze of ancestral amnesia. The folks from AfricanAncestry.com had provided a little more clarity but still no individual identities were known. Now we had much clearer picture about the matriarch of our maternal line in America. For the first time, I could see all the way back to Africa, and through her to Polynesia and Southeast Asia.

When I googled the common surnames of descendants of Virginia's Malagasy slaves, I gasped. Names such as Carter and Byrd popped up. These weren't just familiar from popular culture, they were the names of some families to whom my grandma had been closest for generations. We came off neighboring plantations, went to the same churches, and vacationed at the same beaches. It felt as if tribal ties had disappeared from our knowledge, but a greater gravity still held us together in the same orbit.

Then there were Gates's revelations about my grandmother's European ancestors. "Every English and French king back to Edward the First and Charlemagne's grandfather?" I knew my dad descended from French royals too, maybe English ones as well. Did this mean my Black Mom and White dad were cousins via some royal court in Europe?

Finally, there was that bit about us and our cousin Maggie Bland all descending from President Thomas Jefferson's grandmother. It's not hard to hear echoes of his preamble to the Declaration of Independence in my grandmother's insistence on our perpetual freedom.

One could say that his "All men are created equal with certain inalienable rights, among these are Life, Liberty and the Pursuit of Happiness" is just a long way of saying "Never forget our people were always free." And after all, in the context of the eighteenth-century monarchy, saying that every royal subject has a natural right to liberty is just as revolutionary as saying in its American colony that every enslaved man and woman is free. While the lawyer may quibble, as a person of faith my grandma conceded no ground when challenged on the logic. We are all made in God's image. Every child of God is born free. What man does from that point on may be legal, but that doesn't mean it can't be an abomination, let alone contrary to God's law. It's the logic of every slave rebellion. It is the logic of every colonial rebellion. It is the logic of the American Revolution itself.

The ultimate antidote for the insanity that is racism is to deepen our knowledge of self and understanding our national and ethnic origins. A White guy coming to understand that his background was Irish accelerated his healing. Now that my family knows we descend from Afro-Polynesian pirates on one side of my mom's family and the Limba people of Sierra Leone on the other, our ability to heal from the inherited trauma of slavery accelerated, too.

11

A FORGOTTEN
HISTORY OF RACE

I sat there listening to four men in a small-town English pub talking about the "four races." The more they talked, the more I wanted to walk over to them and say, "Y'all just need to chill. Where I'm from, y'all White." But I'd been at Oxford for six months. I knew better.

Five months earlier, I had volunteered to become a bartender at my college bar. The first night, I poured beer like we did in American college frat houses and the bars nearby. I slammed down the tap. The beer splashed against the bottom of the glass. The head spilled over the side. People stopped talking and stared. I flipped the tap back up. It did not go over well. The English mostly hate foam. They insist the top be so glassy you can stare straight through to the bottom of a pint glass of lager. I adjusted. Conversations resumed.

On the other hand, Guinness confounded me. The slightest amount of speed made it grow foam. Once it had a head, it never subsided. Ugh. By the second night, I was banned from pouring Guinness indefinitely. Humiliated, I was now fully committed to learning the subtle art of pouring the world's most popular stout.

To learn, I began crawling through Oxford pubs and sitting at the bar, striking up conversations with bartenders, learning the fine art of pouring stout slowly yet efficiently. One night I sat in one of the oldest pubs in Oxford, from a time when humanity was shorter. Anybody like me who was more than six feet tall had to duck from the moment they entered the bar until they left.

I couldn't help but notice a raucous conversation at the first table, closest to the bar. The four old men were sitting around, talking about the inherent nobility and abilities of some races and the inherent vice and shortcomings of others. No, they weren't talking about any combination of the groups cited in such debates in America: Blacks, Latinos, Whites, Asians, Pacific Islanders, and Native Americans.

No, they were scrutinizing Irish, Scots, Welsh, and Anglo-Saxons. They described the Scots as greedy and overly fixated on money, a stereotype eerily familiar to the ways in which many people have attacked Jews for centuries. They characterized the Welsh as wild, unruly savages, reminiscent of the stereotypes used to slander Native Americans. The Irish they characterized as slothful, prone to vice, and dumb, stereotypes that echoed the portrayal of Black people in the English press, which historically depicted two groups of people as monkeys: people of African descent and the Irish. And well, when it came to the White Anglo-Saxon Protestants like them, they were clear that they were the apex of humanity.

As I sat there in the bar, it struck me: *race* is an ancient word for tribe. The noun "race" entered the English lexicon by way of the French in the mid-1500s. The French borrowed the word from the Italians who originally coined the term *razza* for "kind, type, or genus." We Scots are a mighty race. We Irish are a mighty race. We English are a mighty race. We Welsh are a mighty race. It's all right there in the Oxford English Dictionary. How come I hadn't realized that before?

Barbara Fields taught us the history of the South at Columbia University. She used the conquest of the British Isles to illustrate how the approaches to managing Native Americans and enslaved Africans in the Americas evolved from earlier conquests and subjugations of other populations.

When the English arrived to conquer Scotland, reports came back from the field that there were two types of natives in Scotland: enlightened ones who recognized the inherent superiority of the Anglo-Saxon upon sight and agreed to collaborate in their colonial ambitions; and savages who acted the way an Englishman might if you suddenly proclaimed that his house was yours.

The geniuses at Oxford and others who advised the Crown reasoned that the difference between the two was a matter of blood. Civilized Scots should be rewarded with land and high positions. Savage Scots should be controlled at all costs, interbred at every opportunity, and killed as required. Differences in their constitutions was a matter of blood. And the only true way to civilize a savage population was, ultimately, to mix their blood . . . through rape.

This is analogous to the approach the British took toward African slaves. British slavers were unique among their European peers. They systematically raped female slaves from the day they were boarded onto the ship. Undoubtedly, many of the sailors took pleasure in it, but their officers also encouraged it because they saw blood mixing as a key strategy for creating a management class, a group of slaves who would be half civilized and half savage.

There were other strategies, too. When the Anglo-Saxons arrived in Ireland, reports came back to London that there were no civilized natives in Ireland. They were all savages. And so the order went out: exterminate them and replace them with the teeming hordes of London. The tensions that exist between Irish Catholics, who exemplified the historically native population, and Irish Protestants, typical of the immigrant English population, go back to the original Crown plans for Irish genocide. The strategy deployed against the Irish mirrors the strategy used against Native Americans when Native Americans proved impossible to subdue into slaves.

Professor Fields's short history of the *rehearsals* for American colonialism and slavery reminds us that much of what the Europeans did in the Americas, they first did to one another. And yet slavery in America evolved into a unique institution. Throughout European history, enslaved people were always seen as fellow humans of nationalities that had lost wars or had been otherwise targeted for subjugation. Populations were stereotyped, and oppressed through the institution, but never was their basic humanity denied.

So it was in America, in the beginning. Professor Fields's research showed that during the 1600s, Africans were categorized by nationality on the slave rolls at each port.[1] For instance, human traffickers would document, "We picked up twenty Guineans at this port, sixteen Senegalese at that port," and so forth.

Yet, a hundred years later, slave rolls denied Africans their humanity altogether. They were not listed by nationality; they were listed as beasts. We picked up five cattle, six chickens, and twenty Negroes at this port, and so forth. What happened?

What happened, Professor Fields reasoned, was the rise of a hateful ideology masquerading as "science."[2] As the scientific revolution in Europe flourished, modern racism was created to order all of God's creation.

In short, the original European notion of race categorized humanity into different geographic groups. The "modern" notion of race created by Europeans and American colonists in the 1700s divided humanoids, in descending degrees of humanness, from the most "superior" human (Anglo Saxon Whites) to the "missing link" between man and monkeys (Negroes).

In other words, although *race* is an old word in our language, *the institution of race* as we know it is relatively young, barely older than our nation itself. (You may notice that in this book I have chosen to capitalize all racial categories. The reason is simple: I don't know any people who are truly black in color, and I don't know any people who are truly white in color. These are labels that refer to categories originally established by law. Thus, I have chosen to treat them as proper nouns.)

In the beginning in America, Professor Hamilton reminded us, there were not slave rebellions, there were colonial rebellions. People of different colors and nationalities bonded together across the thin wall between slaves and indentured servants.

African slaves and European indentured servants worked together in the colonial enterprise. They also began to increasingly rebel together against their colonial overlords.

Indeed, three hundred years before the 1963 March on Washington when a multiracial coalition flooded Washington's National Mall to demand equal rights and economic justice, the first such rebellion occurred not three hundred miles away. That day, a group of working men in Gloucester County, Virginia, made a stand based on class, not race. We often ask whether Martin Luther King Jr. would recognize the world today but it is equally valid to ask whether he would have recognized the world of 1663, when Black and White children of slaves and servants played together in the tobacco fields.

The Gloucester County Conspiracy, also known as the Servants' Rebellion, marks the first recorded instance of African slaves and European indentured servants rising up together for justice against the ruling elite.

The Conspiracy took place at a time when Virginia growers depended on both slaves and indentured servants to farm tobacco. Management treated their workers with cruel abandon, regardless of color.

Unwilling to accept their fate, a group of Black and White workers met in secret to plot a revolt. After securing weapons and a drum to call others to join them, they planned to "march from house to house" until they reached the mansion of the royal governor, Sir William Berkeley. Once there, they would demand their freedom and resort to force if necessary.

The plot failed. Tragically, their conspiracy was outed by another servant who was rewarded with his freedom after the conspirators were caught, some hanged, their plot shut down. However, the rebellion tapped into something important for us to consider in today's context: people can work together across color lines to create a fairer, freer society. Indeed, our core interests demand it.

The ultimate failure of the Gloucester County Rebellion was memorialized as a "holy" day in colonial Virginia because the governing elites wanted to convince the masses that interracial cooperation was futile. The elites didn't stop there. After that rebellion, governing authorities accelerated the colony's transition to slave labor, phasing out European indentured servitude altogether. They were terrified of the possibilities, and power, of the solidarity of working people, and identified race as a necessary dividing line. The failure of the Gloucester Rebellion marked a turning point because from then forward, European elites increasingly leveraged racism as a tool and structure to consolidate and preserve their class power, under the guise of White supremacy.[3]

The landowners also recognized the power that Gloucester's European indentured servants and African slaves would possess if they banded together. It scared them. Additional rebellions, including the more famous Bacon's Rebellion, in 1676, left them filled with terror. The specter of servants and slaves—and according to some accounts, Native Americans as well—rebelling together ignited a profound fear in the minds of colonial elites and authority figures who governed America. Howard Zinn describes this: "Only one fear was greater than the fear of Black rebellion in the new American colonies. That was the fear that discontented whites would join Black slaves to overthrow the existing order. In the early years of slavery, especially, before racism as a way of thinking was firmly ingrained, while white indentured servants were often treated as badly as Black slaves, there was a possibility of cooperation."[4]

Zinn goes on to quote Edmund Morgan, who further characterizes the perceived dangerousness of intergroup/interracial cooperation: "There are hints that the two despised groups initially saw each other as sharing the same predicament. It was common, for example, for servants and slaves to run away together, steal hogs together, get drunk together. It was not uncommon for them to make love together."[5]

The landowners devised a strategy to stop such rebellions. Over the next several decades, they fomented racial contempt between the European and African members of the underclass by pitting them against each other. On the plantation, that meant giving the Europeans nominal control in the field. At the level of the colony, it meant permitting European indentured servants to join the militia and carry firearms. Eventually, it would also include forbidding African slaves from wearing European dress, and requiring them to wear homespun cloth to make it clear to anyone who saw them they were a slave and nothing more. As Edmund Morgan explained, the landowners devised racism as a device for control and manipulation.

The rebels in Gloucester recognized what King memorialized in his famous remarks on the National Mall: we are, by our nature, capable of great things when we judge one another on the content of our character, not by the color of our skin.

Race relations in America began with shared struggle, not mutually assured destruction.

I return to Professor's Hamilton's lesson: politics is a lot like physics. For every action, there is an equal and opposite reaction, and objects in motion eventually return to their original state. In other words, if the original state of race relations amongst working people in America—witness the earliest colonial rebellions, starting with Gloucester—is one of unity, then it follows that moving beyond our nation's twisted notion of race and legacy of racism is not just obtainable, it is inevitable.

Very few Americans truly understand that race as we know it is a literal science fiction created just a few decades before the American Revolution began. Tragically, the way that fiction is woven into the fabric of our nation has cost us, all of us, dearly ever since.

It infects our psyche. It infects our politics, it even tears families apart. And in the process, it holds our nation back in ways that are so profound that it's hard to wrap our minds around it.

Yet the physics of politics gives us a reason to hope that we might actually return to an original state where nationality, ethnicity, and culture are all appropriately important, and where racism—the very American tradition of denying the full humanity of people of a darker hue—does not exist. In the process, we would be free to finally achieve the destiny that Frederick Douglass saw for all of us: To be "the most perfect example of the unity and dignity of the human family the world had ever seen." Let us each commit to deliver that day.

12

POLITICS AND BETRAYAL IN BLACK AND WHITE

Race has a way of making good people blind to big problems. Sometimes that seems theoretical. In other moments, it is utterly palpable. In 2008, it was a bigger factor in the circumstances that precipitated the Great Recession than most knew.

Four years earlier, the NAACP had gone to Capitol Hill demanding a moratorium on housing foreclosures, pointing to the greed-fueled outrages of the mortgage industry. My colleagues were told, in summary, "It's terrible what's happening in your community, but we can't make special legislation to address that." Many in Congress, apparently, thought that Wall Street's greed would remain fixated on Black people forever rather than understanding that we were merely the canary in the coal mine. If you ignore a dead canary in a coal mine, let alone a flock of them, the whole thing will eventually explode.

When we allow racism to cloud our vision of the poor, more Americans suffer than most realize. A nation that imagines most of the poor to be Black loses sight of the Whites who actually make up most of the poor. In the process many White political leaders let millions of their White constituents go hungry every year.

The scholar john powell observed an even more detrimental parallel phenomenon. When the victims of social ills as portrayed in the media look like the majority population, public support for addressing those ills is high. When they look like a minority population, public support plummets.[1]

He discovered the phenomenon by looking at media representations of the impoverished during the Great Depression and at the height of the civil rights movement. During the prior era, poor people were depicted as White and support for anti-poverty action was at an all-time high. Since the latter, low-income people have been depicted typically as people of color, and public support for safety net programs has plummeted.

The same phenomenon repeats across Western democracies. When images of poverty shift from those who look like the majority population to those who look like minority populations, support for public investment in impoverished communities plummets. In this way, the creation of racism has not just devastated Black communities, it has also devastated low-income White communities.

The biggest group of welfare recipients has always been White people, and yet, in the public imagination, they are overwhelmingly Black. White conservative politicians lead movements that slash welfare and hurt more White people than Black people. Similarly, they imagine drug addicts to be Black when most are White. As a result, they underinvest in drug rehabilitation, hurting both communities deeply and the White community often in bigger numbers.

The solution, of course, is simple. When it comes to ending suffering—be it poverty or addiction—show the faces of the afflicted. Don't play to stereotypes, just let the images of America's suffering in its full diversity tell the tale. When people see others who look like them among the suffering, it is harder for them to deny their humanity. If we speak more honestly about these issues, the public will be more likely to support interventions that actually fix the problems, and one by one our neighbors will start to thrive again.

I also knew those facts underscored the truth behind the criticism that we had become the National Association for the Advancement of

Certain People. The recession provided an opening for us to move decisively back toward our roots of simultaneously fighting racism and also combatting the original colonial evil that birthed slavery: unchecked greed and human exploitation.

I took the reins of the NAACP on September 15, 2008. In the midst of the final push to turn out votes for the upcoming presidential election, the recession hit hard. The staff was terrified. The organization's budget had been cut in half over the past two years. They had seen half of their colleagues let go. I convened the entire staff in the chapel at headquarters. With everyone assembled, I stepped up to the microphone.

"I know you've all heard the news," I started. "Let me assure you of two things. One, we will not be laying anybody off. As long as I'm here, we will only add to the strength and numbers of our staff. I've already raised the money to get that started. Two, given that the recession has started, we will need to make some changes in our programs.

"Currently, our economic programs are focused on housing, equal accommodations, and promotions inside corporate America. In each case, you have to be a solid member of the middle class to benefit. From this point forward, anything new that we do will be at the nexus of the most pressing civil rights crises of the day and the ongoing urgent need to end poverty in America."

The need to fight racism and poverty simultaneously is hard to escape in places like Baltimore. There was no way I could. The NAACP headquarters was less than three miles from the housing projects where my mom spent the first half of her childhood. Many families were still stuck there. I was keenly aware that 48 percent of Black America was in poverty the day Dr. King was assassinated, and 48 percent of Black America was still in poverty forty years later.

Few staff members questioned whether fighting poverty would be a distraction.

There is a populism running through the NAACP. It is often as hard to see at the national level as it is hard to ignore at the local and state levels where our units are often frontline allies to trade unions and battles to increase funding for public education in the poorest places in the country. State NAACP leaders such as Rev. Dr. William Barber, Hazel Dukes, Gary Bledsoe, and Ed Dubose exemplified that tradition during my tenure. Our chairman, Julian Bond, walked in that groove with the steadiness of a man who knew his father had helped cut it.

That tradition, like the NAACP itself, is rooted in the post–Civil War leadership of Black leaders and White allies working mightily to uplift millions of recently freed slaves.

I explained it was a resurrection of a tradition. We were born to stamp out the progeny of slavery. Yes, that was racial discrimination. It was also the utter exploitation of the poor. That's how legendary NAACP organizers like Roy Walters and Walter White came to cut their teeth both fighting against peonage and the convict lease system and for the right of workers to organize. That work had among other things led the NAACP to discover and help the federal government to shut down the last slave plantation in the country just before the United States entered World War II. Folks got quiet and got on board. Change is always easier to swallow when it's framed as a reviving or extension of an old tradition.

The populist bent of the NAACP is reinforced by the fact that the very shape of the organization was inspired by nineteenth-century anticolonial battles in Ireland.

The NAACP was originally convened in response to a call made in an editorial by Oswald Garrison Villard, publisher of *The Nation* magazine and the *New York Post*. For a brief period, he even served as editor of both publications simultaneously. His grandfather William Lloyd Garrison was a leading abolitionist and fearless supporter of Frederick Douglass.

Villard's father, Garrison, helped Douglass travel to Ireland when he was still on the run from his slave masters. Once there, Douglass gave speeches to build the international movement against American slavery. With the money and support he earned from speechmaking abroad,

Douglass eventually secured his freedom before returning home to the United States.

Douglass's message was instantly well received by the Irish. After all, St. Patrick had come to Ireland as a slave and the national identity was rooted in the fight to end it on their own shores.

Douglass left Ireland both with the purchase price for his freedom and the blueprint for building a mass civil rights movement, including our hallmark mass meetings made famous by Dr. King. Douglass learned the latter from the Irish Catholic liberation leader Daniel O'Connell. Douglass kept Garrison apprised of his activities while abroad and shared this observation in one of his letters:

> I have but just returned from a great Repeal meeting, held at Conciliation Hall. It was a very large meeting—much larger than usual, I was told, on account of the presence of Mr. O'Connell, who has just returned from his residence at Derrynane, where he has been spending the summer, recruiting for an energetic agitation of repeal during the present autumn. . . . The meeting had been in progress for some time before I got in. When I entered, one after another was announcing the Repeal rent for the week. The audience appeared to be in deep sympathy with the Repeal movement, and the announcement of every considerable contribution was followed by a hearty round of applause, and sometimes a vote of thanks was taken for the donors. At the close of this business, Mr. O'Connell rose and delivered a speech of about an hour and a quarter long. It was a great speech, skillfully delivered, powerful in its logic, majestic in its rhetoric, biting in its sarcasm, melting in its pathos, and burning in its rebukes. Upon the subject of slavery in general, and American slavery in particular, Mr. O'Connell grew warm and energetic, defending his course on this subject. He said, with an earnestness which I shall never forget, "I have been assailed for attacking the American institution, as it is called, Negro slavery. I am not ashamed of that attack. I do not shrink from it. I am the advocate of civil and religious liberty, all over the globe, and wherever

tyranny exists, I am the foe of the tyrant; wherever oppression shows
itself, I am the foe of the oppressor; wherever slavery rears its head, I am
the enemy of the system, or the institution, call it by what name you will.
I am the friend of liberty in every clime, class and color. My sympathy with
distress is not confined within the narrow bounds of my own green island.
No—it extends itself to every corner of the earth. My heart walks abroad,
and wherever the miserable are to be succored, or the slave to be set free,
there my spirit is at home, and I delight to dwell.

   Mr. O'Connell was in his happiest mood while delivering this speech.
The fire of freedom was burning in his mighty heart. He had but to open his
mouth, to put us in possession of "thoughts that breathe, and words that
burn." I have heard many speakers within the last four years—speakers of
the first order; but I confess, I have never heard one, by whom I was more
completely captivated than by Mr. O'Connell. I used to wonder how such
monster meetings as those of Repeal could be held peaceably. It is now no
matter of astonishment at all. It seems to me that the voice of O'Connell
is enough to calm the most violent passion, even though it were already
manifesting itself in a mob. There is a sweet persuasiveness in it, beyond
any voice I ever heard. His power over an audience is perfect.[2]

During his time in Ireland, Douglass watched as O'Connell built a
mass movement against the English occupation of Ireland. He also saw
the movement sustained on the revenues of a penny-a-year membership
and a diet of mass meetings. Douglass brought those lessons home and
helped shape the thinking of the American movement for abolition
and eventually the nascent civil rights movement that emerged during
and after the Civil War. The membership model O'Connell pioneered in
Ireland would later take root in the NAACP upon its founding as well
as South Africa's African National Congress, which was modeled after
the NAACP just three years later.

   In this tradition only one thing really matters: winning real results
in real time. After all, when your neighbors' families, not to mention

your own, are facing real problems, what other choice does any real leader have?

The man who led my family into the NAACP was just such a leader. His name was Edward David Bland. He was born into slavery and would have to beat a White conservative Democrat also named Bland in the general election. That Bland, like Maggie, was a cousin from the slave-owning side of the family. Back then the connection was much more intimate and high stakes.

The humiliation of losing to a man who even looks likes those your family used to own is a volatile thing. After all, another one of my Black relatives who served in the Virginia Legislature during Reconstruction—Peter G. Morgan—gave an impassioned speech at the state capitol only to have his son shot by a former Confederate colonel in retribution. I cannot imagine how frustrated the White Bland in that race was to lose to Edward David.

Edward David Bland had another dangerous fight to deal with before he could even be certain he would be on the ballot. One in his own party.

Throughout the first decade of Reconstruction, White Republicans generally had been consistently courageous allies of their Black Southern peers.

Then the Old Confederacy threatened to secede again.

In the presidential election of 1876, the Electoral College declared Rutherford B. Hayes the winner. Old Confederate leaders insisted their Democratic Party candidate, Samuel Tilden, had actually won. They threatened to restart the Civil War if he was not named president. Mainstream media called what happened next the Hayes-Tilden compromise.

Black people and their most courageous White allies called it betrayal.

The Compromise restored former Confederates' right to vote, shifting the balance of electoral power back to the very Whites who had attacked the federal government in their drive to secede from the United States and maintain legal slavery.

The Compromise also unleashed White supremacist terrorists across the South. Why? Because it greatly shrank the presence and role of federal troops in the South and required all Black troops to be ejected from the region.

Still, even as the stench of massacres filled the air, failure for freedmen was not an option. Ultimately their movement was focused on expanding economic and educational opportunity to those who had been locked out by a plantation-based economic system erected by the state's wealthiest residents. Prior to the Compromise, the Republicans—a coalition defined by relatively wealthy and educated Northern transplants called "Carpetbaggers" and local Black people who together had comprised the majority of the Reconstruction-era Virginia legislature—established free public education for children in the state.

Now that they had been re-enfranchised, many of the wealthiest leaders of the former Confederacy were building a movement to defund and destroy that nascent public education system. These far-right conservatives said the state simply could not afford it because it had to repay its Civil War debt to the federal government.

It had cost a lot to put down the Confederacy's rebellion, and the federal government thought it only fair that Southern states pay for some of it. Southern conservatives, though, used the federal government's insistence on collecting their states' war debt to help build resentment against local Republicans and consolidate a base for the Southern Democrats who were rapidly regaining control of the region.

However, it also masked a deeper conviction of the old plantation elite: education was dangerous because it made workers of all colors less docile and more demanding of fair treatment.

Still, there was a problem: free public schools and other similar Reconstruction-era reforms were benefitting working-class Whites too, and they knew it. These populist former Confederates built a movement of White men who worked the land and the mills across the state. Their party, the Readjusters, broke from the Democratic Party, which was led and financially fueled by local elites who built a base with White supremacist rhetoric and violence. Like the indentured servants who rebelled at Gloucester, the Readjusters' goal was ultimately greater economic opportunity for themselves, their families, and their children. The old plantation owners who led Virginia's Democratic Party in the late 1900s responded as their ancestors had: they sought to destroy the Readjusters by appealing to White unity and supremacy.

The Readjusters responded to the times too. The years that followed the Civil War were economically volatile, and harsh. President Lincoln upended U.S. monetary policy, which before the war pegged the nation's currency to reserves of gold and silver. Instead, to finance the war, Lincoln printed "greenbacks," which were not backed by gold or silver deposits but rather depended on the credit of the United States. It was a system, devised as an emergency measure, that echoed today's Federal Reserve, which relies on the "full faith and credit" of the United States to sustain its national currency.

The printing of greenbacks fueled a boom in the railroad industry that would continue well beyond the war. Between 1863 and 1873, the industry laid 35,000 miles of new track across the country, with railroads emerging as the nation's largest employer after agriculture. The good times didn't last: Wall Street speculation brought it all crashing down. The large infusion of greenbacks, which totaled hundreds of millions of dollars, drove bankers to take unprecedented risks because they were working in a system flush with cash for the very first time. More and more banks borrowed money to invest in innovative and emerging industries, railroads chief among them.[3]

But the railroad business was a speculative one: it depended heavily on government direction and investment, which wasn't always clear or forthcoming. While the railroads were laying tracks at record rates, property rights were in flux in large swaths of the country as settlers, indigenous people, and land speculators battled for territory. If those disputes went unresolved, work stoppages on the railway, or the abandonment of railroad lines altogether, followed suit. It all came to a head in 1873 when the nation's largest railroad financier—formerly the Union Army's preferred financing partner—closed its doors. Jay Cook and Company borrowed too much money to fund its ambitions in the railroad business and eventually, it could no longer meet its payments.[4]

The bankruptcy of Jay Cook and Company on September 18, 1873, echoes in reach and impact the collapse of Lehman Brothers on September 15, 2008—135 years later, almost to the day. The incident triggered the Panic of 1873, which started as a "run on the bank" in city centers and culminated in the nation's first "Great Depression"—an economic depression that would stretch until the end of the decade and impact the livelihood of every single American.

Those were hard years for working families. With the railroad industry in retreat, working people struggled to find work. Unemployment reached historic levels. Consumer demand collapsed and financing for small businesses was virtually nonexistent. Businesses and farms of all sizes collapsed.

During this time, populism as a political movement gained traction. Leaders like Edward David Bland realized that Wall Street speculation and Big Business sold out working people because of their insatiable desire for profit. They also realized that without education, they would *always* be beholden to Big Business and the larger forces of capital to feed their families. After living through nearly a decade of economic collapse, Bland, like many populists emerging in his time, sought out likely and unlikely bedfellows to build the political coalition necessary to change things.

In the Readjusters, Bland saw an alliance to be built. He reached out to the Readjusters' leader, the populist railroad magnate and former Confederate General William Mahone. That action likely did not come easy.

As a seventeen-year-old boy, Bland trudged through the blood and over the corpses of his White cousins to gain his freedom. As a man he looked into the eyes of his fellow Black freedwomen and freedmen and saw their dreams of opportunity and the fear that their hope was for naught.

Then he took a moment and listened to the Whites who shared their economic dreams and struggles, their hopes of education and opportunity for their children, and their fears that greedy elites might steal it all from them. He saw a possibility.

Then he remembered: These were the very men among whose ranks were those who had raped enslaved women. These were the very men who had savagely beaten men like him. These were the very men who fought to keep him and all his people in slavery. And who was their leader? None other than General Mahone.

To local Blacks, Mahone was to the Battle of the Crater what Custer was to the Battle of Wounded Knee. First, he overwhelmed Union troops in a way so clever he said killing them was as effortless as a "turkey shoot." Then, when dozens of Black Union troops surrendered, he massacred all of them.

And yet, having accounted for all of that, Bland also recognized that wealthy Whites like the cousin he would face on the ballot were stoking the flames of White supremacy to fuel their political comeback. Their building wave had unleashed a terror so great that many who had believed in the dream of a New South and a united America were shrinking before it. Top of the list: the national leaders of his beloved Republican Party who had signed that damn compromise with the Democrats and agreed to leave Southern Blacks like him without the protection of federal troops.

Given all the givens, an alliance with Mahone made a lot of sense. They shared political goals for their people. Moreover, it was the last shield left between Bland's people and the Ku Klux Klan.

Beyond ruthless in war, Mahone was a renowned tactician in business and politics, and he saw promise in the proposition. Mahone was a leading businessman in the South's railroad industry, but as the South's economy was devastated from the war, he was struggling to hold on to his business. He needed political influence to lower the cost of capital, revitalize the busted railroad industry, and bring federal investment back to the states of the former Confederacy. Unless something changed, Mahone, and other former Confederates just like him, would struggle to find their future in the restored nation. Something needed to give.

So Mahone and Bland came together to create an uneasy alliance that led the Black voters of Virginia en masse to support the Readjusters. The result was a majority Black party led by a former Confederate general turned populist business mogul that united working-class voters across racial lines behind a pro-working family, pro-public education, and pro-civil rights agenda.

The Carpetbaggers were instantly outraged. My great-great-grandfather did not really care. After all, how could he? His White Republican colleagues were Northerners of means who could always flee the rising racial violence and return to their old homes above the Mason-Dixon. Given that their leader, President Rutherford B. Hayes, had unleashed said violence it was up to men like Bland to keep their people physically safe and on a road to greater opportunity.

Their one hope was their White peers. These men and their families had a lot to lose too. They needed the free public schools as much as Black families did. They needed a state government that would lift all the people from the bottom up rather than return to prewar patterns of simply favoring the rich.

Bland's White Republican peers still had a trump card. He was up for election. They rushed to the courthouse to get him off the ballot and replace him with another candidate.

He and his newly formed multiracial populist movement were already literally one step ahead. When the Carpetbaggers arrived at the Dinwiddie Courthouse to file to replace him on the ballot, they discovered it full of boisterous men, Black and White, united by Edward David Bland's candidacy and the alliance he and Mahone were building. It was clear the Carpetbaggers were outnumbered. What is more, like him and unlike the Northern transplants, most of his supporters made their living working the land. If there was going to be a fight that day his side clearly had the numbers and the muscle to win.

The Carpetbaggers relented. Bland stayed on the ballot as the Republican candidate. With the support of local Black voters and more than a few working-class former Confederates, he soundly beat his White plantation-class cousin.

That year, the Readjusters won major gains in the state legislature, and would go on to secure a majority twice. They also controlled the councils in cities such as Danville and Petersburg, and their control of the state legislature empowered them to elect a governor, the former mayor of Petersburg, and send William Mahone as well as Harrison Riddleberger to the U.S. Senate.

The Readjusters eliminated the new poll tax that was designed to keep low-income people—disproportionately but far from exclusively newly freed Blacks—from voting. They outlawed the public whipping post from Virginia's town squares. They chartered the Virginia Normal and Collegiate Institute, now known as Virginia State University—the first state-supported Black college south of the Mason-Dixon.

Their focus on repealing the poll tax that had suppressed the votes of Black and poor White men alike was smart. By ensuring access to the vote, no matter one's class or race, the Readjusters hoped to sustain the power of their movement for years to come. After all, the Readjusters' class-based, multiracial political coalition had gained significant momentum: in just a few short years, the party controlled the governor's mansion, the state legislature, and city councils across the state, as well as two U.S. Senate seats.

But it wouldn't last. In October 1883, a group of twenty-eight White businessmen published and circulated widely a complaint, "Coalition Rule in Danville," a broadside attack on the biracial politics of the Readjusters.[5] The circular lamented the rise of Black political and economic power. It complained about the fact that the city council

had appointed four Black police officers to the city's force of nine—
"something before that time unknown to the history of the town."

The circular also lambasted the fact that the local market leased
twenty of its twenty-four stalls to Black entrepreneurs, complaining,
"The market, once occupied in all its stalls by polite white gentlemen,
with their clean white aprons, and the most inticing (*sic*) meats and
vegetables upon their boards, is now the scene of filth, stench, crowds
of loitering and idle negroes, drunkenness, obscene language, and petit
thieves."[6]

The businessmen behind the circular went out of their way to stir up
racial resentment. "Negro women have been known to force ladies from
the pavement," the signatories wrote, "and remind them that they will
'learn to step aside next time.'"[7] Although the circular was widely con-
demned as nothing but falsehood, it succeeded in raising racial tensions
in Danville. Just days before the election, two White men opened fire on
an unarmed group of Black people, ultimately killing four of them and
one White person. The violence shook the city.

"Uppity" Blacks, empowered by the success of the Readjusters in
the city, were blamed and scapegoated. Their party was soundly defeated in the election, and Bland and many others lost their seats. As
the Democratic Party regained control of the General Assembly and
local city council, the Readjusters saw their political movement collapse, virtually overnight. Their defeats marked the end of political
reconciliation between the races in the state of Virginia for generations. It was a harbinger of things to come across the South and the
United States: the era of Jim Crow.

In the years ahead, the Democrats would move swiftly to consolidate
their power in order to prevent the Readjusters, or another political party
just like them, from emerging. Poll taxes were passed and segregation was
reintroduced across Virginia, doubly inhibiting any future multiracial
populous movement. Their work culminated in the 1902 Constitutional
Convention when State Senator Carter Glass (who would later go on to

serve as treasury secretary for Woodrow Wilson) rallied his party to institutionalize poll taxes and other means of voter suppression in the state's constitution. On the floor of the state senate, Glass called upon the Virginia legislature to "eliminate every Negro voter who can be gotten rid of, legally, without materially impairing the numerical strength of the white electorate."[8] In practice, the voter suppression that followed the amended constitution reduced the Black vote by 80 percent and the White vote by 50 percent.[9] More than defeated, the multiracial populous was disenfranchised.

It would be decades more before any kind of political cooperation between Black and White people, reminiscent of the Readjusters, re-emerged. Still, seeds for the New Deal coalition that would come to define America in the middle twentieth century had been planted deep.

13

SERIAL (KILLER) MISTAKES

Nothing highlights the dangers of America's racial fixation more powerfully than a look at our history of failing to stop preventable atrocities committed by terrorists and serial killers.

When I was a student at Oxford, Professor Hood and I discussed the pernicious security failures inherent to racial profiling. He explained there was an alternative. The alternative was to focus on what people do, not what they look like. It's as simple as that, and yet as hard as breaking any old habit.

In 2000, George W. Bush won the presidency on a platform that included ending racial profiling and passing comprehensive immigration reform. Tragically, he abandoned both in the wake of the 9/11 terrorist attacks.

The battle to end racial profiling took two massive blows: the president abandoned the cause, and the number of Americans who were targets of profiling increased massively. Law enforcement scrutiny of every American who was Muslim, Sikh, Hindu, or a Christian from the Middle East or South Asia went through the roof. As it did for anyone who looked even vaguely like they might be from the Middle East or South Asia. I found myself suddenly being repeatedly frisked at airports again. The only other time that had happened to me was during the first Gulf War.

I decided I needed to go back to organizing. I took a job launching Amnesty International USA's U.S. Domestic Human Rights program. Yes, you read that right: USA, U.S., and Domestic all in the name of one program. The name was awkwardly repetitive for a reason: across Amnesty International's fifty-five national organizations, across its global movement, there was no precedent for a *domestic* human rights program. This was the era of the United States being the world's "sole superpower." It would take U.S. citizens to police the U.S. government on human rights abuses at home. And in America, that often means matters of race.

I began setting up our campaign to fight racial profiling.

Guided by a young criminologist on my team, Dr. Niaz Kasravi, we dispatched human rights observers to federal "Special Registration" sites. That program was as dumb as it was discriminatory. Immigrants from several predominantly Muslim countries and North Korea were being required to register with the federal government. The lines were long. People would routinely lose wages, even their job, trying to comply. Meanwhile, it was a safe guess that no terrorist was complying. We were humiliating honest and hardworking new Americans and giving al-Qaeda new fodder to use in their recruiting. Dumb just got dumber.

We traveled the country listening to victims of racial profiling. We heard stories of Black professionals being humiliated in front of co-workers, Native American men being humiliated on their way home from religious events, and Latino and Hmong American kids being humiliated in front of their friends. These stories would break your heart.

In Los Angeles, we found our first group of White victims. They were stock traders who lived south of the city. They had to be at their desks between three and four a.m. every weekday. They'd cut through the overwhelmingly Black and Brown neighborhood of South Central

LA on their way to downtown when they were running late. These White guys in their fancy cars kept getting pulled over for small stuff like an expired tag, an unused seatbelt, or a bum headlight. Then they'd get the question: "What's a guy like you doing in a place like this at two thirty a.m.?" *Trying to get to work on time, officer,* they would explain. "Then you won't mind if I search the vehicle?" the officer would shoot back. "Any White guy here at this hour must be buying sex or drugs," the officers always appeared to presume and sometimes said it out loud. Suddenly, these White professionals were in a spot most Black men know well: either you say yes and you're late for work or you say no and things might go sideways.

Their experience put a privileged spotlight on a simple truth: racial profiling runs on the flawed logic of race out of place.

Louis Gray, a Native American survivor of racial profiling in Oklahoma, spoke from the perspective of the first Americans targeted for their appearance, and to the anxiety and pain experienced by all Americans who have suffered such abuse. "From my position, the threat and humiliation of racial profiling appears to be an everyday experience for the Oklahoma Indian. . . . Life for Native Americans is built on institutionalized racism."

In the midst of finishing our report, the unthinkable happened again. And again. And again. For days and weeks, terrorists were loose in and around the nation's capital city killing our neighbors in cold blood.

If you lived in the DC metropolitan area in 2002, you remember just how disorienting it was. We were getting survival advice on the nightly news: if you are going to a big box store around the beltway, you should zigzag when you walk in the front door. If you are pumping gas: dance; it's harder for them to aim at your heart that way. Helpful, but still . . . we were all desperate to know who the suspectes were. The police really seemed to have no idea. So they put out a profile.

A profile is used in the absence of a description of a specific suspect,

and is a series of educated guesses. It typically starts with the probable; it ends with the possible. In this case, it started with: The suspect is
probably antisocial. (Makes sense. They keep killing people.) They are
probably traveling alone or in a small group. (Makes sense. If they were
in a large group, they probably would've been caught quickly.) They are
probably military trained. (Well, they are very good. Makes sense too.)
And they are probably male, and probably White. (Wait? What? Why?)

It turns out that in this country, the racial profile of a serial killer or
lone gunman has historically been a White man. Some say the phenomenon is related to higher social isolation among Whites due to higher prosperity and earlier suburbanization. People who are more socially isolated
tend to be both more suicidal and antisocial in some ways. Some say it's
due to higher numbers in our society and the military. It is also related
to the fact that murders, and thus serial killers, in the Black community
were ignored by American law enforcement for centuries. Suffice it to say,
as long as Black folks were killing each other, most police forces were not
very interested in the cases for most of the years our nation has existed.

One morning two weeks into the terrorism of the DC snipers, a
buddy of mine from work arrived at the office at the exact time I did.
This was odd. I lived nine blocks away from Amnesty International
USA's Washington, D.C., headquarters. There was no traffic but foot
traffic between me and the office. I arrived most mornings at 10 and
left around 9 most evenings. However, Jared lived in Roanoke. He drove
from there to Capitol Hill every Monday and went home every Friday to
see his wife and kids before coming back up to make a paycheck.

Jared and his wife were my kind of Christians, in the way that counts
most: they believed that Jesus came to uplift the poor and built their ministry on that understanding of our savior. They were also more intense
about living their faith than I was. His wife was homeschooling more
than a basketball team's worth of kids to make sure they were raised in
the faith. They didn't let them watch TV, only videos from their massive
library of movies and shows.

Once, Jared said he had the perfect class to tempt me back toward preparing for the ministry myself. I asked him, "And what's that?" "Preaching with rattlesnakes!" he responded, and he was serious. I was nonplussed. "They bite and their bites kill."

"Only the sinners," Jared continued. I reminded him that the Good Book tells us that we are all sinners. He went quiet. I raised an eyebrow and went back to enjoying the Indian food we vacuumed up once a week.

On Mondays, he arrived promptly in the office at 8 a.m. However, DC is the kind of city that gets started around 10. Not for Jared. He always came up extra early from Roanoke to beat the worst of the Beltway traffic. But this Monday was different. Jared was walking in late behind me, as were one or two other White men.

"Nice to see you're finally with the program!" I smirked at Jared. We had started at Amnesty on the same day and had been buddies ever since. He tried to smile back before testifying, "Ben, I can't lie, I'm a little shook. It was the most insane thing."

"I know," I said. "Another shooting this morning. Once again, they took off the weekend. Once again, they start killing us during the Monday morning rush hour. They're a bunch of sick . . ."

He cut me off. He often would cut me off when I was about to cuss.

"It's terrible. But something else happened. Right after the shooting, the dragnet went up. The cops waved me over. Told me to get out. So I get out and I'm standing there on the side of the highway with my hands in the air. I look to my right, there's a bunch of White guys like me, I look to my left, there's a bunch of White guys like me. . . ."

I cut him off this time. "Brother, you have just been racially profiled. Let's have a beer at lunch and talk about it."

That afternoon, I was back from our lunch sitting at my desk staring out the window when something unusual happened again. A White windowless cargo van was cruising past our offices on Pennsylvania Avenue toward the U.S. Capitol when it was suddenly surrounded by six police cruisers. The sirens blared. I went to the window. Twelve officers pulled their guns out. Eight Latino day laborers got out of a van that appeared to have only two bucket seats. They looked totally innocent and completely bewildered.

Our resident PhD criminologist joined me at the window. "All that for an apparent seat-belt violation?" I asked Dr. Niaz Kasravi.

"No. They expanded the profile this morning," she explained. "White van. They got a tip: White man in a white van."

"Huh. White man, white van. It rhymes," I observed.

"Doesn't sound right to me," she shot back. "Too obvious for so many killings."

My godbrother Dave Chappelle had a different take.

A couple days earlier, we were hanging out in probably the safest place you could be: a basement comedy club in a brick building in downtown DC. We were far away from the typical shooting sites near the Beltway, which rings the city. It was also the weekend, and the snipers always did their killings during the workweek.

Since we were young, I have occasionally played the role of the straight man for Dave's jokes.

In the middle of a setup for a joke he stopped and yelled, "Hey, Ben!"

I said, "Yeah, Dave?!"

He said, "I figured out who did it."

"Who did what, Dave?"

"The DC snipers, Ben! I figured it out!" He paused. Dave's a formally trained jazz musician. Most big punchlines are on a downbeat. "They're Black, Ben!" The room got quiet.

"Why, Dave?"

"Because they're taking off the weekend, brother!"

He was just getting started. "Think about it! White psychopaths don't take off the weekend. Jack the Ripper. The Boston Strangler. Dudes like that . . . Man, the weekend is when they do their best work!"

The crowd roared with laughter. The tension had been building for more than a week. The jokes were totally inappropriate, and yet right on target. We all needed the catharsis. That's why we go to comedy clubs. They provide the safest form of inappropriate relief you will ever find.

"But a brother. . . . A Black psychopath. Well, brother . . . A brother might just take off the weekend." We all sat in silence for a moment and then burst out laughing. It was apparently the first real joke any of us had heard about the snipers, and we were still in the midst of their reign of terror.

That's the unique beauty of my godbrother's comedic mind. He can literally find a joke where no one else can and deliver it when everybody needs it. Here's the obvious thing about Dave: he is a bona fide genius from a family of such. Dave's dad went to Brown University at fifteen. His mom was a translator for famed Congolese freedom fighter and Prime Minister Patrice Lumumba and was one of the first Black women ordained in the Unitarian Church. His great-grandfather was an AME bishop, one of America's early Black university presidents, and a leader of national renown. Dave is smarter than most people I know. It's wise to pay attention to the truth behind his jokes.

In the club, Dave started from the observed *behavior* and worked his way toward *race*. In the streets, the police were starting at *race* and working their way toward *behavior*.

And our neighbors kept getting killed.

Then, when it was over, it turned out Dave was the only person with a microphone in all of DC who had had it right.

The killers, John Muhammad and Lee Boyd Malvo, were Black. They were driving a blue car. The "possible" end of the profile was way off. They were far from White. So was the tip. However, the police's top-of-the-list descriptors—the probabilities—were spot on.

Antisocial? Check. In addition to the boy sniper clutching the Bushmaster and ammo in the trunk, there were other signs. They were showering only once a week, at the Silver Spring YMCA. (Located on the Beltway, since just after the shootings it's been the only YMCA in

America where you cannot buy a day pass.) Thus five days out of the week they would have likely had bad body odor. Hygiene is the first thing to go for most people who become psychotic.

Military trained? Check. John Muhammad was wearing a military jacket with his name on it.

Alone or in a small group? Check. There were just two of them, and Lee would often stay in the trunk so he could shoot through a hole in the back of it.

Shortly after the arrest, Chief Charles Moose of the Montgomery County Police came out and said that they had stopped these guys almost ten times before they were arrested.

Almost. Ten. Times. And they never searched the car. They never walked the perimeter of the car with a dog trained to sniff for gunpowder. They never opened the trunk. They never asked, "Hey, what's this hole cut into the back of your vehicle?"

It's worth noting that law enforcement's belief during the DC sniper manhunt, and in many places to this day, that serial killers are almost certainly White men is itself a product of Jim Crow racism.

Modern criminology is generally said to have been shaped and defined as a field by Emile Durkheim. It has existed only for roughly a century and a half. For most of that time, segregation existed in America. And for virtually all of that time, the legacy of slavery and Jim Crow has influenced the policing patterns of American law enforcement.

As James Baldwin outlined in his last book, *The Evidence of Things Not Seen*, murders in the Black community have been serially undercounted and underinvestigated. As a result, Black serial killers have largely gone undetected. As it was in South Africa during Apartheid, as long as Blacks killed each other in their own neighborhoods, historically American police did not spend much time investigating. Thus, the historical "facts" about who American serial killers are and what communities they come from are themselves an artifact of Jim Crow law enforcement patterns.

That is what happens when you insert race into the equation, the blinders go up, we forget we are all Americans, criminals go uncaught, and more people die needlessly.

And other people, like my friend Jared, were humiliated, shaken, and late for work.

In the midst of all that, something else was happening at our local airport—Thurgood Marshall Baltimore Washington International (BWI).

( )

Do you remember Nathaniel Heatwole?

Don't feel bad. Nobody remembers Nathaniel Heatwole. He was a student at Guilford College in North Carolina, traveling on a short flight from Raleigh every week to do research in Baltimore. He started to notice at a certain point that he was not just on the same flight every week, he was on the same plane with the same tail number.

At some point, he left a box cutter in his backpack and didn't remember it until he had passed through security. It was the same thing used as a weapon used by terrorists to take over planes during the 9/11 attacks, and no one had spotted it and no one had stopped him.

He thought it strange, disturbing even.

Meanwhile, guys like me—the ones of many races and nationalities who look vaguely Arab to your average airport security person—were getting frisked every single time. Every time I would ask why. Every time I was told it was random. Eventually I asked, "Could you hand me my ID, officer?" The officer said, "Why?" "I just need to check if there is a typo. Apparently, my new name is 'Random.'" He frowned. I frowned back and raised my eyebrows.

Back to Nathaniel. The next week, he left the box cutter in his pack again, and again he went through security without getting stopped. Then he said, well, let me put a couple more in there, and see what happens. And he went right through.

So then he took it to the next level. He took some modeling clay that resembled plastic explosives—but actually wasn't—and put that in his backpack. And it went through security, no problem.

Then he thought, "If I'm on the same plane every week, I'm going to go into the bathroom and jimmy open the vanity. I'm going to tape box cutters inside it, and see if they find them."

Meanwhile, Nathaniel would see guys like me, light-skinned Black, Puerto Rican, Middle Eastern, having the same conversation every flight.

Nathaniel didn't know if he was more scared or angry, but he knew something was very wrong. After all, it was reasonable to assume that al-Qaeda–aligned operatives like the would-be shoe bomber Richard Reid and the "dirty bomb" conspirator José Padilla were recruited specifically because they were not Arab nor from the places targeted by the post-9/11 Special Registration policy. Nathaniel's sense of urgency built up so much that he did something. You can debate how smart it was, but you can also admire his sense of right and wrong.

He wrote a note saying this is my name, and this is where I live, this is who I am, and this is what I've done on this date and that date, and this is what you haven't done. He attached it to the backpack with the box cutters, and he left it in the overhead bin on the plane.

They found it and read the note. They opened the vanity and found the contraband.

Then they arrested him.

You look at these cases, and you think to yourself, well, maybe our perceptions of gender and race being what they are, they're just hard-wired. Maybe we will always be inclined to see men as more dangerous than women, people of color as more dangerous than White people. Maybe there's no getting beyond this.

Then you remember Squeaky Fromme.

( )

Squeaky Fromme is famous because she took a shot at President Gerald Ford. For two hundred years before that—this was right around the time of the bicentennial—the orders of the president's bodyguards had been essentially: "Keep an eye on everybody, but focus on the men. Do not worry about searching purses. Women don't shoot at anybody."

How many minutes do you think it took after a woman took a shot at Gerald Ford for the Secret Service to say, "Oh, we better check the purses, too?"

Do you remember which president's life was saved by checking purses? George H. W. Bush's. President Bush had a rally, and a woman showed up with a pistol in her purse. The Secret Service by this point had been checking purses for twenty years—and they found the pistol.

One might say, "Okay, well, if we can evolve when it comes to sex, maybe we just need a racial Squeaky Fromme. Maybe if we had a racial Squeaky Fromme, we could kill racial profiling, at least in the domestic security context, at least when it comes to protecting presidents."

If you search throughout history, you'll find that we actually did have one—three quarters of a century before Squeaky Fromme.

In 1901, President William McKinley was shot and killed in the assassination that elevated Vice President Teddy Roosevelt to commander in chief. President McKinley was shot twice at point-blank range by an assailant carrying a pistol in a crudely faked bandage, wrapped in gauze. The president would die a week later from a series of medical errors as his doctors struggled to treat the wound.

When the trigger was being squeezed a third time, somebody in the crowd tackled the assailant to the ground, and the bullet glanced off to the side. It was a critical intervention. The abdomen is full of big blood vessels, so a third bullet to the gut almost certainly would have killed the president quickly.

The Secret Service agent in charge of the overall operation ran over to the agent in charge of the rope line to find out what had happened.

The protocol for the line was simple. Back then, they did not have metal detectors. The instructions to his men were straightforward and easy: search everybody head to toe as they entered.

The supervisor was likely upset. If his men were doing what they were supposed to do, no one could have walked up to the president with a gun in their hand wrapped in thin cotton and shot him point blank. What happened?!

His agents had two explanations: first, the shooter looked like any other mechanic with a bum arm out for a day at the fair. The killer was blond, blue eyed, average height, and clean shaven. They didn't squeeze the bandage because they did not want to hurt him.

Second, they believed the shooter had a decoy, because they had rushed the short blond man with the bandage through so they could focus on the gentleman right behind him. He was swarthy, about six feet four, and boasting a very long mustache.

Why was that last statement important? Because the ethnic or racial profile of a presidential assassin at the end of the nineteenth century and the beginning of the twentieth was based on the killing of a Russian leader by Eastern European anarchists. The anarchists had issued a warning to leaders from the West: you are next.

The authorities didn't have a suspect-specific description, so they put out a profile. The racial and ethnic element of the profile was clear: Eastern European anarchist, likely tall, swarthy, and with exotic facial hair.

The officers then fanned out and found that tall, swarthy man with the very long mustache. He couldn't have been hard to find. Fewer than 4 percent of American men in 1901 were even six feet tall.

There was good news and bad news. The good news? They found him. The bad news? He was Constable Big Jim Parker, the light-skinned, Black, retired Georgia constable who tackled the assailant before the officers on duty could reach him.

It turned out that the short, fair, freshly shaven shooter was an Eastern European American anarchist, Leon Czolgosz. He met the probable profile: he approved of violence and belonged to an anarchist sect. He was even in love from afar with Emma Goldman, the notorious anarchist leader.

But the racial blinders were up. He was not tall, nor swarthy, nor he did he have exotic facial hair. He was allowed to walk through the security checkpoint unbothered, with a gun in his hand, and shoot the president of the United States of America at point-blank range.

It's not as if no one at the time heard this story. Newspapers then were like CNN today. They would tell the same story day after day, morning and night, until it stopped selling. In the morning edition, evening edition of many papers, every day for a week, until McKinley succumbed to his wounds because of bad medicine, there was the photo of Big Jim Parker, the man who saved the president.

The point is this: we knew in 1901 that if you focus prematurely on unchangeable characteristics such as somebody's skin color, their height, their sex, or perhaps culturally common things like their style of mustache, then people can die unnecessarily. The actual perpetrator, whose *behavior* might make them more suspicious but whose physical appearance doesn't conform to the stereotype, can get through because you're distracted.

Our nation's top law enforcement officers knew their men on the scene had been distracted by the profile. And they knew that an assassin succeeded in killing the president because of it. And yet they did not change their protocols the way they did after Squeaky Fromme. They still have not.

Simply put, U.S. law enforcement's fixation on race often makes all of us less safe when it matters most. My neighbors in DC, Maryland, and Virginia kept getting killed by two Black psychopaths while the cops pulled over my White colleagues. The White Oklahoma City bombers slipped out of town while the cops looked for Arabs. And the officers protecting President McKinley allowed an Eastern European-American anarchist to walk their rope line with a pistol in his hand wrapped in cotton because they were distracted by the hue and facial hair of the man behind him. A century later, the 9/11 terrorists shaved their beards to arouse less suspicion, just as terrorists had done in Algeria decades earlier.

Ultimately, the threat posed by racial profiling is to all of us and to our nation as a whole. It humiliates the innocent and drives them to hate institutions they once admired. It distracts law enforcement and leads them to inadvertently give terrorists a predictable formula for greater success. Terrorists and psychopaths have always come in every color.

More recently, the internet has made it increasingly easier for them work together across those lines and even divisions of ideology.

The day our law enforcement agencies stop focusing on the common biological and cultural factors of color, hair, and faith and start focusing exclusively on criminal behavior is the day we will all be a whole lot safer than we are right now.

14

ONE IN THE WHITE HOUSE, ONE MILLION OR TWO IN THE BIG HOUSE

T he operative phrase in the NAACP is double A. We are not the NAAACP. We are not the National Association for the Advancement of A Colored Person. We are the National Association for the Advancement of Colored People. Last time I checked, we had one Black man in the White House and a million in prison. As far as I can tell, sir, we have a lot more work to do."

It was the end of the NAACP's centennial celebration in 2009. I was speaking at a press conference. We had just hosted the forty-fourth president of the United States. No one could imagine anything more poetic than Barack Hussein Obama being sworn in less than a month before the nation's greatest civil rights organization turned one hundred years old. As a former journalist, I always try to answer reporters' questions earnestly and honestly.

"Your organization, sir, the NAACP, the National Association for the Advancement of Colored People. One question. Now that there's a Black president, how much further do your people need to advance?"

That question again and again and again, every day for a hundred days. I was done. It was time to make it plain. We had a lot more work to do. Of course, the election of Barack Obama did not signify the end of racism in America. The other purpose of how I answered that question was to make it clear that ending mass incarceration was now on the agenda for the NAACP.

The day after President Obama addressed our Centennial Celebration, I picked up the *Daily News* downstairs at the hotel. Errol Louis had covered the event. The end of the story caught my eye:

> It was inspiring, of course. But as even Obama's most delirious Black supporters are learning, the President is too busy working the levers of power in a troubled, turbulent nation to take on the symbolic title of Black-Leader-in-Chief or Ambassador on Racial Matters.
>
> That leaves the NAACP in its traditional role as the conscience of the nation—and particularly of the powerful—on confronting poverty, crime, racial profiling and economic discrimination.
>
> Benjamin Jealous, the new president and CEO of the NAACP, says the organization will focus on the myriad factors that land a disproportionate number of Black men in prison.
>
> "We will be judged by our grandchildren on how we deal with mass incarceration," he told the Daily News editorial board last week.
>
> Jealous, a criminologist by training, knows he's leading the NAACP into a complex maze that includes the external injustice of racial profiling and the internal culture of violence that festers in many low-income communities.
>
> But he's clear that the future of civil rights lies in tackling tough issues, a fact not changed by the election of Obama.
>
> "We have one Black man in the White House and a million in prison," he often says, making it clear who counts the most for the NAACP. [1]
>
> The one man from the White House gave a businesslike description of how he plans to inject federal dollars into the best and most innovative inner-city schools, paired with boilerplate about how even the poorest families must uphold standards of personal responsibility.

In the process, he downplayed one of the NAACP's priorities, the battle against the payday lenders, rent-to-own companies and others sharks that lure low-income families and communities into crippling, high priced credit traps.

But that didn't faze stalwart NAACP-ers in the slightest. Jealous, celebrating the group's 100th anniversary, has already set his sights on the long term.

"You have to be willing to practice discipline for decades," he said.

In other words, he said, last night marked a historic milepost on a much longer journey.

Our message was getting through. And our lane was clear.

Michelle Alexander would popularize the term mass incarceration months later with the release of her book *The New Jim Crow*. We were both rooted in the same broader activist family of criminal justice advocates. We had all used the term for years. And yet, when I used it as president of the NAACP, many reporters would put it in quotes, like it was a strange idea.

The problem of mass incarceration in America is so big you can see it from space. It's always like that when it comes to the great human rights atrocities facing Black people in America. They're always so big you can see them from space. You could see slave plantations from space, with their large swaths of land cleared by Brown backs bent over, picking cotton. You could see Jim Crow's ghettos from space, Brown bodies pushed into overpopulated urban centers. And now you can see America's prisons pockmarking the landscape from sea to shining sea.

It's easy to racialize the problem of mass incarceration. Civil rights lawyers love to talk about disproportionality. They focus on the percentages, and with good reason; the percentages are outrageous. Black Americans are the most incarcerated people on the planet.

And yet, as organizers, we try to change the laws not by appealing to a body of nine judges, but rather by building a majority consensus in city councils, state legislatures, and the U.S. Congress. We deal in numbers, not percentages. And for us, it's relevant to know that we don't just have a million Black men in prison, we also have a million White men in prison. Moreover, women of every color are the fastest-growing demographic behind bars.

Simply put, America doesn't just have the most incarcerated Black or Brown people on the planet, we also have the most incarcerated White people on the planet.

With roughly a million Black people in prison and roughly the same number of White people in prison in the United States, you might say, "Well, the Black population is much smaller." It's true. The rate of incarceration for Black people is much higher. But understand it in these terms: a Black man in the United States today is three times more likely to be incarcerated than a Black man was in South Africa at the height of apartheid, when that country led the world in incarceration.

It is *also* true that a White man in America today is almost as likely as the average Black man in South Africa, at the height of apartheid, to serve time behind bars.

As I once said to my (White) father, "Dad, you know that if White privilege in America in the twenty-first century only buys you a twenty to twenty-five percent discount on the incarceration rate of Black men in South Africa at the height of apartheid, then we're all in the frying pan. When the only question is whether you are on the edge or in the middle of the pan, everyone should be clear that we are all in the pan!

( )

In short, not only do opponents of mass incarceration have our work cut out for us, we also have a whole lot of families to organize.

When the pain of mass incarceration is concentrated in one's own community, it is often hard to see beyond one's own experience. Then, one day, God sends you a sign that you need to adopt a broader view. That sign came to me when I stepped onto a plane in Atlanta. I was flying Delta Airlines to Memphis, Tennessee. I flew so often that they automatically bumped me up to first class. And it's first class, so even though it's 11:00 in the morning, the first question you are asked is "What would you like to drink? Bloody Mary, bourbon?"

"No, ma'am. It's eleven a.m., ice water will be fine."

"Yes, right away, sir."

As the flight attendant moved toward the head of the cabin to grab my water, a passenger sat down next to me. He was wearing a bright red shirt with a Confederate flag over his heart. I craned my neck to make out the tattered stitching over the flag. It was hard to read from my angle. He saw me staring at his shirt and stretched out his hand. "Hi, I'm Bill."

"Nice to meet you, Bill. I'm Ben."

"Great day, isn't it?"

"Yes, it is, Bill."

"Tell me, Ben, what do you do?"

"Well, Bill, I'm the national president of the NAACP."

"Well, golly," Bill said.

The waitress arrived with my water. I looked at her and smiled. "Ma'am, I'll take that bourbon after all."

"Tell me, Ben, I mean, would you mind just answering one question for me?"

"Sure, Bill, what is it?"

"Tell me this, what's the purpose of affirmative action?"

"Well, Bill, the purpose of affirmative action is to destroy nepotism as the operating system for our country."

"Hell, Ben, you can sign me up for that. But tell me this, what good does that do for the boys in my family?"

"Well, Bill, let's start with the basics. Do you have a wife? Do you have daughters?"

"Sure. I got both."

"The impact that affirmative action has had on women in America is undeniable. Their earning power, their career prospects have been transformed."

"I get that, Ben. Maybe you don't get me, sir. We don't worry about the women in my family. The men on the other hand, the boys, well, they've been in and out of prison since we came here on the wrong side of the Georgia penal colony. Me, I was the anomaly in my family. Still am. I was a great football player when I was in high school. Got me a scholarship to the University of Mississippi. That's why I wear my old booster shirt."

I remembered Johnny Reb and the Confederate flag used to be the pair of images that represented the university.

Bill continued, "Well, the coach took a liking to me and introduced me to business executives up in Memphis. One of them gave me this booster shirt. He also gave me a career. Well, every now and then I fly back home to check on everybody down here in Georgia. But I made my career up in Memphis because I got that football scholarship. And every time I fly home to Memphis from where I grew up, I'm troubled by the fact that the boys and the men in my family stay stuck. So tell me, Ben, what does affirmative action do for the men and boys in my family?"

"Well, Bill, I got to tell you, it does a lot at the university level. Most universities don't just apply a gender or race lens, they also take a geography and a class lens. They give extra weight to applicants who are the first generation to attend college, and those who come from impoverished geographies that typically don't submit many applications to their universities."

I continued, "I suspect you're talking about employment. And when it comes to employment, well, all I can say is that I agree with President Obama. Our companies shouldn't just be using a gender lens and a race lens when it comes to affirmative action. They should also overlay the class lens."

We talked for a few more minutes, and just as quickly as our conversation started, it ended. Turns out the flight from Atlanta to Memphis isn't very long. As I walked off the plane, I realized I should have talked to him about mass incarceration. After all, he had mentioned the Georgia penal colony. That gave me an idea.

President Obama's administration had its hands full. The recession was taking a real toll and already dragging down the president's approval rating. It was clear that if the issue wasn't healthcare or jobs, it was unlikely that any significant domestic legislation was going to get through Congress anytime soon.

I picked up the phone and reached out to Newt Gingrich. He responded quickly and said that he'd be happy to talk. When we connected, he said he shared our concerns and expressed that he'd be happy to team up in some way. Emboldened, I picked up the phone and called the antitax activist Grover Norquist. He, too, was open.

What's more, after 2010, White incarceration rates had surged as American law enforcement shifted their focus from urban Black communities to rural White communities as they transitioned from the war on crack to the new war on meth. That shift wasn't a mistake. It resulted from having hit "peak oil" in the war on crack and pressure to keep their numbers up.

The war on drugs incentivized American police departments to keep arresting more and more people. It was a strategy as misguided as the reliance on body counts to determine whether we were winning in Vietnam. The logic was circular and led to nowhere good. It worked like this: If your local police department was going to receive enhanced funding from the federal government to fight the war on drugs, it had to prove two things. First, is there a present need? And second, are you making ongoing progress?

Both need and success were measured in the same way: the number of drug arrests your officers were making. The largest group of crack users in America had always been middle-aged, middle-class White men. However, enforcement against this population was difficult. They tended to live in relatively large houses surrounded by relatively large yards, and it was very difficult to detect what was happening inside their homes, let alone their basements. Even when the police sought to enforce the law, it was very likely that the inhabitant had the means to hire a lawyer.

On the other hand, in urban Black communities, people live in tight small spaces stacked on top of one another: apartment buildings and housing projects. Crack is smoked, which produces a noxious smell, not unlike cigarettes, and just as with cigarettes, people had a tendency to smoke it by an open window or even on the fire escape. If they smoked it in their apartment, the fumes leaked out into the hallway. Even if an officer messed up, the chances that a Black low-income resident would hire a lawyer were about nonexistent. For all of these reasons, and more, detecting crack use in America's inner cities was like shooting fish in a barrel.

Therefore, the police profited by focusing on our communities. After decades of sustained enforcement, there simply weren't enough Black crack addicts to arrest, so the police shifted their gaze toward meth addicts. And they moved from housing projects to trailer parks, from urban areas to rural areas, rounding people up like we had done in tenements with Black folks in the war on crack. And in the process, the number of American White men behind bars skyrocketed.

As a result, this country became the world's leading incarcerator. Prior to that, it was the former Republic of South Africa. Prior to that, it was the former Soviet Union. It is worth noting that both nations no longer exist. Each had been destabilized by internal stresses exacerbated in part by the high costs of incarcerating a huge percentage of the domestic population.

Social scientists have studied how mass incarceration is tantamount to "forced migration," removing a proportion of a community's residents and leading to imbalances in the ratio of men to women. Across the world, men are ten times more likely to be incarcerated. At home, women endure the costs that stem from the removal of men from the community: less social cohesion, higher incidences of sexually transmitted diseases, and a collapse of economic and job prospects.[2]

The United States was now in a similar position. What is more, it was getting worse by the day. In 2000, White men here were half as likely to be incarcerated as Black men in South Africa at the height of apartheid; by 2010, they were three quarters as likely, and Black men more than twice as likely.[3]

Nevertheless, Americans are so confident in the relative strength of our nation that they can't imagine mass incarceration destabilizing it the way the Soviet Union and South Africa were destabilized.

When President Obama showed up at the NAACP's Centennial Convention, he didn't even mention the problem. It disappointed me a little. I knew that he knew just how big a problem it was. Senator Jim Webb of Virginia championed the issue in the Senate when Barack Obama served as a senator. When I first learned Obama's name, I was an organizer working on related issues for Amnesty International, and he was a state senator in Illinois who had championed criminal justice reform.

Something had to be done. The pain and pressure on other issues created by mass incarceration was too significant to ignore. Fortunately, a movement was building in the states.

( )

"Books not bars!" "Books not bars!" Students at Berkeley revolted late in 2009. The university was imposing tuition for the first time, and the students were outraged. They understood that this would result in many of them ending up deep in debt. They investigated how this had happened, and what they ran into was another price of mass incarceration.

Simply put, America's prisons were eating the lunch of America's public universities every day, and had been doing so for forty years.

In 1970, California's prisons represented 3 percent of the state budget, and those institutions were reserved for the most dangerous people in the state. By 2010, the public universities had shrunk to a mere 7 percent of the state budget, with tuition rising to almost $9,000 annually. The prisons, on the other hand, had surged to consume 11 percent of the budget. They were filled not only with the most dangerous people in the state but thousands of the state's homeless, drug addicted, and mentally ill, as well as thousands of others who had committed nonviolent offenses.

The "good news" was that California's public universities had not fallen to the level of investment once occupied by the public prisons. The bad news was that prisons received 50 percent more funds than the universities.

It was clear that the state's education budget was being cannibalized by its prison system. Let's be honest, in the public's imagination, it's always somebody else's kid who is going to prison. It's always our kids who are going to college. On some level, the resistance to putting the full burden of mass incarceration on public universities symbolized our love for our kids and our belief that our kids deserved investment. But when you looked at the numbers, the surge in funding for prisons appeared to have no end in sight, sending a very clear signal. As much as we loved "our kids," there was something that trumped that love—our fear of "somebody else's kids."

During this time, we hired a brilliant researcher named Monique Morris to lead the NAACP's research department. I asked her to pull the budget histories of multiple states. Every state we studied told the same story: In 1970, prison budgets were small, and the prisons were filled with dangerous people. From 2010 to 2020, the prison budgets were bloated, and the prisons were stuffed with nonviolent offenders and drug-addicted people who should have been in rehab. In Pennsylvania, New York, and Georgia, it was the same story. Indeed, we couldn't find a major state with a substantially *different* story.

Moreover, in 1970, all state universities were either tuition-free or had nominal tuition fees. By 2010, the cost had surged in every state. Student debt surged alongside fees, as did student debt default rates. When you looked closer, you couldn't help but notice something else.

Every single child in America was or would soon pay a price for mass incarceration. The young people behind bars are paying a price. The young people in college are paying a price in higher tuition. And the young people not in college because it had become too expensive were paying a price too—one that you could measure in dollars, because the single best way to increase your earning power in America is to go to college. For those who don't, it may feel like you're saving money, but it will cost you far more in the long run.

And yet, with Republicans controlling the states with the largest prison populations, I was stuck for months on how to break through. And then I met Bill on Delta Airlines.

It occurred to me that his history sounded a lot like what I knew about Newt Gingrich's family. I also remembered that Newt was a college professor. And when we got into it, he wholeheartedly agreed with what we were attempting to do. He agreed to write a two-page letter of endorsement. With that, I knew our prospects had changed tremendously. Grover Norquist fully agreed that America's prisons needed to shrink, and yet being Grover, he wasn't prepared to give a dollar to anything with the word *public* in it. He agreed to endorse the first half of the report.

Before we went public on the PBS news hour, we looked at Grover and said, "Hey, why don't we just talk about the half we agree on?" Grover was game. "It's fine with me."

Given the rising strength of the Tea Party insurgency, the endorsements of Grover Norquist and Newt Gingrich virtually guaranteed that we would meet a receptive audience in every capitol in America. The NAACP supporters would read the report, the Tea Party supporters would read the letter. Either way, we would communicate our point and grow our coalition. It turned out that it was the moderates in each party who were opposed. They were generally addicted to donations from the prison lobby and afraid of changing anything. We didn't pay them much attention.

By organizing state legislators aligned with activists in both the Democratic and Republican parties, the NAACP and the Tea Party, we formed a majority to overwhelm the moderates in every state.

That fact might be hard for some people to wrap their minds around.

How was it that the Republican activists were so eager to line up with Democratic activists on an issue as controversial as criminal justice reform? To understand that, you have to understand the composition of Republican activists at the time.

The Tea Party was like Neapolitan ice cream. It was a combination of three flavors of activists. The first were libertarians, the second were conservative Christian evangelicals, and the third were fiscal conservatives. Libertarians had long-stated concerns about America's drug laws; they literally could not understand why you would incarcerate anybody for a crime they were committing against their own person.

Christian conservatives were typically aligned with prison ministries that were right on the front lines of America's mass incarceration epidemic. At the time, there were approximately as many White men behind bars as there were Black men. The inmates were coming almost exclusively from families that were already financially stressed. More importantly, in most prisons, upwards of 90 percent of inmates of all colors were too poor to afford their own lawyer.

And the ministries that served them understood the deep damage that mass incarceration was doing to their families, to their children, to their economic strength. In short, for this group of conservatives, the need to end mass incarceration was especially urgent.

That left the fiscal conservatives, who often lacked courage on this issue. And yet, if you had the backing of the libertarians and the Christian conservatives, you had their full attention. After all, their goal was to shrink the state budget, full stop. In private, they would often admit how to cut corrections spending had confounded them for decades. When the NAACP presented them with a plan endorsed by the likes of Gingrich and Norquist, they quickly got on board.

It turned out that many Republican governors found the mix of flavors of support irresistible. Often, this was for deeply personal reasons. Sometimes, one would respond that it just made sense, almost as if they'd never thought about the issue before. A son of Governor Nathan Deal of Georgia was a drug court judge, so he was better informed than most. As Arnold Schwarzenegger once told me, he was a bodybuilder, so he had a lot of friends who had been to prison. Governor Rick Perry of Texas didn't seem as interested in the issue, yet each of them stood up to support our efforts.

Nathan Deal teamed up with Stacey Abrams, and they led the state through a wholesale revision of the Georgia criminal code, greatly reducing the number of people behind bars in the state.

The Texas Criminal Justice Coalition, led by the talented organizer Ana Yáñez Correa, former head of the Texas chapter of the League of United Latin American Citizens, put together a coalition of NAACP and Tea Party–aligned legislators that together passed fifty-two criminal justice reform laws in Texas in two sessions. All but two of those were signed by the Republican governor, Rick Perry. The net effect was that it put Texas on track to shut down a dozen prisons. That was a big deal. In the history of prisons in Texas, they had never shut down one. They had only opened new prisons or refurbished old ones.

In California, Governor Arnold Schwarzenegger, also Republican, was very receptive to our push to decrease mass incarceration and make it easier for formerly incarcerated people to find jobs. "I'm a former body builder. I know lots of felons. They all need jobs!" he confided to me with refreshing candor. He removed obstacles to state employment for people who had served their sentences. Then he embraced our call for shrinking prisons by proposing a state constitutional amendment that would forbid the state from ever spending more on its prisons than it did on its universities. California was different from Georgia and Texas in one critical way: Democrats controlled the legislature, and the Democratic moderates were much more powerful than they were in the other two states. We hit a brick wall in the California legislature when the moderates dug in. There was no overcoming them that session, despite our having the support of the president of the prison guards' union.

Mike Jimenez, president of the California Correctional Peace Officers Association, courageously stepped out to help address mass incarceration in California. After all, his members had worked triple overtime for years. He understood two things. One, cutting the state's prison population in half would not cost him one job. That's how big the problem of prison overcrowding had become in the state. And two, he understood that there but for the grace of God go each of us. As Mike said to me, "When I was a young guard, I used to look out on the prison floor and think, what a pity these men didn't have fathers like me involved in their sons' lives. And then one day I looked down on the prison floor and my own son was there. My son, like the loved ones of many of us in this country, struggled with addiction." He knew his son needed rehab, not prison. But at the height of the drug war, all that America had to offer its addicted citizens was prison. Despite the strength of our coalition, the prison industry lobbyists rallied California's moderates and shut us down.

Schwarzenegger was succeeded by the renowned Democratic leader Jerry Brown. In his first year in office, he made a bold proposal of his own: the prison system should receive even more of the state budget and the public university system even less. We had actually gone from a Republican governor proposing a requirement to shrink the prison system or increase funding for public universities, to a Democrat proposing the opposite. [4,5] This was not progress.

It would take a few years, but ultimately, criminal justice reformers in California would find their own way to get around the moderates in the state legislature. The leadership of great strategists like Tim Silard, president of the Rosenberg Foundation, brought the matter directly onto the ballot. California's voters overwhelmingly endorsed it, and finally, the state was on a path to shrink its prison population.

As we built the bipartisan movement for criminal justice reform in America, I was grateful to Van Jones for his early agitation on the issue. He was the first to coin the phrase *books not bars*. It was his framing that those students at Berkeley lifted up in their protests.

As an organizer, I was personally indebted to General Colin Powell. Years before, in one of our first conversations, he told me, "Ben, it's easy to recognize what you disagree with people on. What's more urgent and important in any democracy is to spend your energy figuring out what's the one thing that you can agree on with a political foe. Figure that out and you can get a lot done."

His advice gave energy to our successful efforts to abolish the death penalty for juveniles nationally, and to entirely abolish the death penalty in several states. Now it was our strategy for shrinking the prison systems in Texas and Georgia, and rapidly becoming the NAACP's strategy for criminal justice reform across the country. "As you win one victory together," the General continued, "You might just discover along the way that there's something else you agree on."

15

THE NAACP IN
THE WHITEST STATE
IN THE UNION

Paul Richard LePage was elected the seventy-fourth governor of Maine in 2010. As a city councilor in Waterville, he had developed a reputation for saying things that were racially problematic, and generally being off his rocker. This time, he went too far. He publicly announced that the NAACP could "kiss my butt."

It demanded a response.

Lots of folks questioned how a governor with an adopted Black son could say something like that. I've known plenty of men with wives who are sexist; it didn't surprise me that a White man with a Black son could say something that was racist. What I couldn't get over was that there would be no Governor LePage without the NAACP.

Like the governor before him, LePage was a descendant of French Canadian Catholic immigrants from Quebec. Why is that important? Well, a century ago the Ku Klux Klan was as fiercely anti-Catholic as it was anti-Black and anti-Jewish. In 1920, opposition to the immigration of Catholic French Canadians had driven membership in the Ku Klux Klan in Maine to such high levels that the state was second, per capita, only to Georgia.

The whole thing took me back to the worst part of my summers spent on the East coast. It reminded me of the racist attitudes I had seen old French Canadian tourists display toward me and other Black friends who were also visiting the Jersey Shore. And it reminded me of the way White friends up in Maine would call the Quebecois "Canucks" and taunt them. Rather than inflaming racial tensions, I wished that Governor LePage could see that his people and mine had more in common than not.

We penned a terse public reply. We explained that we only knew of two still-existing groups that had publicly challenged the Klan's persecution of Catholic Quebecois immigrants during its heyday in Maine—the NAACP and the Knights of Columbus. I closed by saying that before Governor LePage stepped down, he should apologize.

At the very bottom of the press release, we mentioned that my family had been in Maine for generations and in New England since 1636. That last bit was erroneous. My father's family had arrived in 1624. It might have seemed like a random flourish. It was not. Maine is an especially provincial corner of New England. No national NAACP president had been there in more than forty years. I knew I would be heading up there soon and wanted any local leaders who saw my comments to understand I was personally invested in the state healing old racial wounds.

Maine was a special project of mine. It was clear the state had been sorely neglected by my peers. While its Black population had always been small, it was no different than many other rural places and small cities where the Association spent more time. The local NAACP president, Rachel Talbot-Ross, was the second person in her family to step up and take on the responsibility. I promised her the first time we met that I would always have her back.

When I arrived in Maine, I on a threefold mission: to help Rachel raise the flag of our organization a bit higher in the state; to assure the growing Somali immigrant population that we would support them, not just locally, but nationally; and to deal with the crisis at the Maine State Prison.

The prison, in Thomaston, was founded in 1824. The old captain's house on the cove in Thomaston once belonged to my great-grandfather. My grandparents and great-grandparents are buried in the local grave-yard, as is my great-uncle who died in a hunting accident while a student at Bowdoin. When we rode into Thomaston, I immediately spotted the old prison store. As a child, I'd often bought wooden trinkets and leather belts there on summer vacations to visit my dad's brothers and mother. And then I noticed the graveyard. I bought two wreaths, one for each of my grandparents, to lay on their graves. I cleaned up their grave sites and laid down the wreaths before heading to the prison.

The prison is an imposing structure from an earlier era. At the time, it housed about one thousand inmates, almost 90 percent of them White, approximately 10 percent Black, and a small number of Native Americans, Asian Americans, and Latinos.

NAACP organizers among the inmates had grown the membership to almost two hundred men, or 20 percent of the general population. However, only half of the Black men in the prison had joined. In other words, of the 200 members, almost 150 of them were White.

That's the Maine I knew as a kid. Governor LePage was a manyfold historical anomaly as far as I was concerned. The inmates of Maine State Prison were more reminiscent of the Maine I had known as a child. And I loved them for it.

When I arrived at the prison, they ushered me in quickly to meet with the men. More than half of the NAACP members were assembled. We went through their grievances. They had many, and many of them were serious. However, there was one issue that was clearly existential for them. The warden had decreed that no civic organization at the prison could have more than fifty members.

The men explained to me that there were only two civic organizations at the prison, the NAACP and the Long-Timers. The NAACP already had two hundred members and was growing fast. The Long-Timers had thirty. Setting the cap at fifty allowed the Long-Timers to grow by 60 percent if they wanted to. Capping the NAACP at fifty would not only stop any future growth, it would cut its existing membership by three quarters, relegating it essentially to being an all-Black organization. The White men were clear that if the governor was going to cut the membership, they would give the Black members the first option to stay in.

I said that was ridiculous. I pointed out that the local NAACP chapters in Maine were half White and always had been. I told them the story of Governor David Cargo of New Mexico. He had started the first NAACP chapter at the University of Michigan Law School as a White Hispanic Republican in the 1940s. When I asked him why he started it, he said, "Well, when I was growing up in the Southwest, the NAACP was the only civil rights organization in town. But those of us who were Brown, those of us who spoke Spanish, we needed it. And when I got to the University of Michigan Law School, well, we needed it too."

"The NAACP is not a Black organization," I said. "We are a very Black organization, and there's a difference. We're just like Amnesty International, but the opposite. They're not a White organization. They're a very White organization."

Everybody laughed.

"That's exactly right. The difference between being a Black organization and a very Black organization is that at the end of the day, we're here for everybody who wants to be part of the organization, and everybody who needs our help." The men applauded.

Then the guards came in and said it was time for me to see the warden. I was ushered into his waiting room and sat on the couch for fifteen minutes. I was familiar with "hurry up and wait." It gave me time to collect my thoughts. The warden entered from a side door. He was dressed to the nines in the finest duck-hunting outfit I'd ever seen.

His jacket matched his knickers. And when he smiled and extended his hand, I noticed that his vest did as well. Over his shoulder appeared his son, who was similarly dressed.

And then I noticed something else. Both of them were wearing the longest L.L. Bean boots I had ever seen. As a child, I would marvel at them in the winter catalog. Who wears those things? Who has time to tie them, let alone lace them? They must have seventy-two eyelets.

Apparently, this is what they were for. The warden noticed me looking at his boots, so I said, "Nice boots. Bean, right?"

"Of course," he responded.

"My dad's family used to make socks for Bean. I'm not sure we ever made them long enough for those boots." He laughed and we sat down. I could see his wheels turning.

"Mr. Jealous, today's my birthday. My son and I are long scheduled to go duck hunting. But honestly, sir, if I had ignored this visit, given that you have organized twenty percent of my inmates, I might have a riot on my hands. So, I'm here out of respect. I hope you will respect that it's my birthday and we can keep this brief."

"Certainly," I replied, "however, before we dive into business, let me just thank you for getting me back to Thomaston."

"You've been to Thomaston before?"

"Yes, sir. I used to come here every summer. You know the old captain's house on the cove?"

He said yes.

"My great-grandfather owned that house for decades. But today, I had a special mission. I laid wreaths on my grandparents' graves. They're in the old cemetery. The one a mile from the prison door."

"I know the one. You said your grandparents are buried there?"

"Yes, sir. And my great-grandparents and my great-uncle."

"So you're a Mainer?"

"No. My parents' marriage was against the law in Maryland and that great-grandfather disowned my dad up here in Maine. I was raised in California, but I came back here as a child every summer to throw dirt clods at flatlanders in the Saco River. (*Flatlander* is Mainer for douchebag. It's most commonly used to describe tourists from Massachusetts.)

He laughed and roared, "Son, you're a Mainer."

I chuckled. "No, my family just used to make socks for Bean, three generations of my family are buried down the road, and my dad was born in Biddeford and graduated from Deering High in Portland. I'm speaking there later today. But no . . ."

"Son, stop. You're a Mainer. Up here, that all counts," he interjected with a smile. "What do you want, son?"

"Sir, respectfully, you know what I want. No limit. Please just withdraw the limit on our membership."

"You've got it. You brought the media with you, didn't you?"

"Yes, they're expecting me when we're done."

"Tell you what, why don't we just go out there and tell them you're a Mainer, it's my birthday, and you're getting everything you want."

I paused. I've never had anybody insist I was a Mainer before. In my childhood, up here I was always called out for not having a Maine accent and then teased when I would slip into one similar to my father's by the end of the vacation. (Meanwhile, back home in California and Baltimore, I was laughed at for saying "idear" instead of "idea," like my father.) It felt good to have a local official of any sort insist I belonged.

More than anything, it felt good to be able to go back and tell the men that they'd got what they most wanted, the thing they needed to stay together as a group.

We had the press conference. It was a big success. On my way out of the building, I bumped into a representative of the local Republican party. He was there to recruit new members, too. Maine and Vermont are the only two states that allow inmates to vote, and it wasn't lost on me that they also had the smallest percentages of citizens of color of any state in the union. Rachel Talbot-Ross, the local NAACP president, mentioned that only the Republicans and the NAACP ever came to register inmates and recruit them. It broke my heart to hear that about the Democratic Party, and yet my heart also swelled with pride for the fearless determination of the NAACP in the northernmost and Whitest state in the union.

16

COURAGE AND SOLIDARITY

O n the way home, my thoughts drifted back to the solidarity I saw among the inmates. I had never seen that sort of solidarity among inmates before, let alone a group so diverse yet so overwhelmingly White. The first time I had seen it was when a lone man came to the aid of one who was already dead.

When the campaign to save Black colleges in Mississippi ended in 1993, I had two job offers, one from the local McDonald's and one from the *Jackson Advocate* newspaper. The one from the local McDonald's came first. It was simple: work an hour a day, greet people at the front door, and they would pay me for eight hours so I could get back to organizing. It was generous but I also knew the owner, Mr. Leroy Walker. He was a shrewd businessman and I worried he would soon weary of the bargain.

The second job offer, I created myself. I walked into the offices of the newspaper and asked to speak to the publisher, Mr. Tisdale. He was fearless and a bit eccentric. The eccentricity I dismissed as the armor necessary to persist. His was the most frequently firebombed newspaper in the United States in the 1980s and 1990s. When I arrived at his office, it had already been firebombed three times in the last fifteen years.

I had gotten lost on my way there and driven past the charred carcass of the previous office. It was riddled with the distinctively large holes left by submachine gun bullets. I shook Mr. Tisdale's hand and told him what I had seen. And then I noticed that the new offices were brick. He laughed, "Yeah, we're a little bit like the three little pigs." I sat down and remarked that I'd noticed he had a job posted for a graphic designer. He looked at me and cocked his head to the side, the same expression my dog makes when he's confused.

"Son, we do need a graphic designer."

"Well, I can do better than the last guy. I saw the paper." You could tell I'd hurt his pride a bit, but he laughed it off.

"But, boy, I thought you could write?" he asked.

"Sir, I don't know where you got that from."

"Well, you went to one of them fancy schools up north, didn't you?"

"Yes, sir, Columbia University. But only for two years, sir, just long enough to get kicked out for protests."

"No, never mind, son. Down here, you can write." And with that, I was hired.

I reported to work three days later, on a Monday. My assignment was simple. "Son, you will need to write two stories every week for the front page. I suggest you figure out your stories today, write them tomorrow, polish them Wednesday morning. Then you'll hand them to the typesetters."

I realized then that this must be the last newspaper in America that had typesetters. Everybody else had computers.

"They will then prepare them for layout." Layout was done with wax and paper. Even the student paper at Columbia had shifted to computers by then.

"Yes, sir. So how do I find a story, sir?"

"Just go outside and listen to the people. They'll tell you what's going on."

He was right. You didn't have to be Columbo to find stories of corruption and abuse in Mississippi. That was my main beat, corruption

and police abuse. It was explained to me that while it hadn't been
posted yet, the position was open because the last reporter was in a
mental hospital. She had allegedly been gang-raped by the officers she
was investigating.

It was my first day as a reporter and I was already on the front line
of American journalism. After the fiasco of my first few attempts at the
inverted-pyramid approach to writing a news story, Mr. Tisdale gave me
two other assignments. "Go to Memphis and get yourself a copy of *The
Guardian*. Read it from cover to cover. Their back issues, get those, too.
Find *The New York Times*, pick that up as well. You're a good writer, but
you need to learn how to be a good newspaper writer. Those two papers
will teach you."

He continued, "In the meantime, we're going to take you off of big
stories for a while, son. We're going to put you on the church beat." Mr.
Tisdale had a rhyme to his reason. He knew that if the pastors knew I
respected them, they would prove to be a fount of great stories for years
to come, and they did. Along the way, I learned to humble myself as a
writer and get the facts right. I picked up some good life advice as well.

One day I was coming to a hundredth birthday celebration for
Mama, the matriarch of Jackson's blues and gospel record industry. Her
eighty-eight-year-old sons had started playing professionally when they
were twelve. Folks said the twins had opened for Robert Johnson more
than once.

The session musicians for the nightclubs and the churches were
the same lot. Mama became everybody's mama because on Saturday
nights when she was getting her boys home to tuck them in bed after
the opening act, she would say to the musicians, "When y'all get done,
y'all just come by Mama's house, and I'll make you breakfast."

When the clubs closed out at two or three o'clock in the morning,
everybody packed up and headed to Mama's house. There she fed them
and got them ready before they headed off to the early morning church

services at 6:00 or 7:00. There was not a woman more beloved in Jackson by those musicians than Mama.

On Saturday, everybody was dressed to the nines. The blues played was distinctively Chicago, and the gospel often blended into R&B. I was doing a pretty good job of keeping all the bands clear in their categories but there were a couple that confounded me. I leaned over to my neighbor in the crow's nest of the church's multipurpose room.

His name was "Cadillac" Sims. He was an old light-skinned bluesman with slicked-back hair and a Cadillac automobile insignia hanging around his neck. When I met him, he saw me looking at it and remarked, "Yeah, I've been wearing that longer than those boys from Hollis, Queens," a nod to Run-DMC.

I smiled. "Cadillac," I said, tilting my head to whisper to my neighbor in the balcony, "please forgive me, brother. I'm an Episcopalian. I thought I could keep all these bands straight, but I'm struggling a bit to tell precisely which ones are gospel, and which ones are blues. I can't afford to only get this eighty percent right. I'm hanging on by a thread at my job. Please help me. How can I be certain who's playing gospel or who's playing blues?"

"Oh, son, it's simple. It's just a matter of tense: Gospel is about the trouble that come. Blues is about the trouble that already done happened." Those words have stuck with me ever since.

If journalism was a band, it was clear the *Jackson Advocate* was a blues band, and our leader, Charles Tisdale, resembled an aging Cab Calloway sitting at his desk, always dressed in an attractive suit, often sporting suspenders. His day consisted of shuttling through the small triangle that was Miss Peaches Soul Food, down the block and across the street, and the speakeasy directly across from our front door.

A few weeks later, I caught him as he was walking back from lunch. He said, "You're back on the beat, son. You've done good." He noted that he appreciated my ear for the language and the bits of wisdom I'd captured from Cadillac. My chest stuck out a bit further. I stood up a bit taller. I had been worried.

A few weeks later, I was sitting at my desk. The one I had chosen was the farthest from the window, in the back corner of the newsroom. Given the paper's recent and frequent history of being firebombed, I figured I wanted every opportunity to escape the flames and avoid being hit. I was also often the last one there, and the arsonists always came at night. One day, while I was sitting at my desk, writing on deadline, Mr. Tisdale walked by, laughing. He dropped Jackson's daily newspaper, the *Clarion-Ledger*, on my desk.

"Flip it over," he said. The headline read, "Six Man-Eaters Captured at Res." I loved Ross Barnett Reservoir. A beautiful place despite being named for a terribly racist former governor of the Magnolia State, and apparently full of twelve-foot long alligators.

"I told you, boy, no Black man should be swimming in no reservoir named for no Ross Barnett." I looked at the map graphic in the lower left-hand corner of the article. The dock it pointed to was the one I dove off when I went for my swims on the weekend.

The article explained that these alligators had grown both extra-large and completely unafraid of men. Worse, they had begun to associate man with food, so they had to be put down. Apparently, all of this had been caused by chicken farmers amusing themselves by hauling their runts down there to feed them like dog snacks to the gators.

Imagine them sitting in the back of their pickup trucks, grabbing the chicken by the neck, cutting it a bit so it would attract extra attention in the water, and tossing it out as they took a swig from a whiskey bottle. I was done swimming at the reservoir. I looked at Mr. Tisdale.

"Thanks for the tip," I said.

"No problem. By the way, I have something else for you." He brought a large box to my desk and plunked it down. The box had weight.

"Son, I don't know what's in this box, but I'll guarantee there's a story. As best as I can tell, it was sent to us by a White woman. Judging by the last name and the city, it's likely the case. But most notably, if you take a moment, you can tell that she had mailed it to all of the dailies in the region before us.

"There's only two possibilities, son. Either there's no story in the box or there's a really big one they're all afraid of telling. You've got a week."

I got a utility knife from the layout desk. I opened the box carefully. It had been taped and re-taped many times. Inside the box was a letter written on lined notebook paper. It was from a mother who said her son was an inmate at Parchman, and his life was in danger.

She said that her son provided evidence of prison guard corruption to the FBI in order to help prosecutors break the code of silence among the guards and to convict their peers who had killed an inmate in cold blood. She noted that we would find a copy of most of the documents in the box. She asked that we call her if we wanted to report on the story or needed additional information.

I contacted the mother right away and arranged to have her son call me. The story that emerged was this. A body of a black inmate had been discovered in a shallow grave just outside Parchman. The problem: no prisoners had been reported missing or killed. The FBI investigated, but ran up against a wall of silence. They couldn't figure out who had killed the inmate or why. Then they caught a break: the prison chaplain had information, but he wanted the FBI to immediately transfer the prisoner who provided it for his safety. The FBI agreed. The chaplain handed over the information. But before he did, he made copies of the papers and sent them to the prisoner's mother. That was the box now on my desk.

The box included stacks of papers. I sorted them into a few piles.

The first was a pile of applications from guards seeking promotions. It seemed clear that each of the successful applications for promotions were frauds; the résumés attached to their successful applications were wildly more impressive than the ones attached to their unsuccessful applications just a few months earlier.

The second pile contained notes from a meeting of officers among the guards, including decisions about who should be promoted.

The third pile included complaints about the head of the canine unit responsible for searching inmates' cells for drugs and other contraband. They showed that the head of the canine unit himself had failed drug rehab five times. He had been reprimanded for buying clean needles from inmates. His girlfriend had been banned from prison grounds after being found shooting up on campus. He still had his job.

The last set of documents were literally homemade receipts of the donation of expensive drug-sniffing dogs from the canine unit to one of the public officials who had recently had responsibility for overseeing the state's corrections system. It did not appear this man had any of those dogs at his home. A criminal defense attorney explained it was likely that the former public official, who had received all these donations while he was still in office, had sold them to drug traffickers. Before they put a car or truck carrying drug contraband on the road, they liked to use these dogs to make sure similar hounds would fail to discover their payload.

The FBI had used the information to break the code of silence, but reneged on the deal. They left the prisoner, Bill Hunt, in Parchman. The other newspapers in the state wouldn't touch the story. Governor Fordice was notoriously vengeful toward news outlets that reported anything that put the state or his administration in a negative light. Newspapers that crossed him could lose valuable advertising by the state. That left us. This was a job for the *Jackson Advocate*.

Whenever we spoke, Bill was fearless on the phone. Yes, he understood the guards were recording every call and likely listening to this one. That was the whole point in his mind. They were fixing to kill him and were less likely to do so if they knew he was talking regularly to a reporter. We ran our first story on the case the next week. Front page headline above the fold. The series continued for more than a month. By the second week, a secretary from the state government was knocking on our front door. We opened it, and she asked for ten copies of the paper. We asked why. We were pleased to sell them but asked why she wanted so many. She said she was taking them back to the legal department at the state Department of Corrections. She added tersely, "Because we are going to sue you and shut you down because of your terrible lies about our guards." I politely thanked her for buying so many copies, and mentioned that the truth was an absolute defense against any charge of libel.

I shut the door behind her and hollered, "They're scared, boys. Let's keep it up."

Not only did they never sue us, we soon had word that the state police had launched an investigation into our allegations of corruption at the state prison.

"The state cops are in here, tearing up the place. Turning over filing cabinets. Looking under every desk. Going through every document." Bill confirmed the rumors with glee.

"That's great, Bill, but I am going to need somebody else to corroborate your stories," I told him.

But I also knew that the threat to Bill's life was real. And Bill was still at Parchman. If they killed him, not only would a courageous man be dead, but we wouldn't have anybody else to corroborate his story, we would likely be in hot water.

I could tell Bill was thinking hard. He had every motivation to help me find another source to confirm his reports. As far as he was concerned, he only had days left to live if we didn't get him out of there fast.

"I think I figured out the answer," he said. He named a specific high-ranking officer at the prison.

"Really?"

"Let me finish. Yes, he is the loneliest man I know. You have to get a woman to call him. She has to be White. She has to be native-born

Mississippi. She can't be from Alabama, and she can't be Black. But if you can find a true Mississippi Belle to give him a call, he will be so tickled. He will answer every question she asks, no questions asked, just to keep her on the phone."

Bill was a fucking genius. He was like Tim Robbins's character in *The Shawshank Redemption*. He had attracted the attention of every officer in the prison by accumulating more college credits than any inmate in the history of Parchman. This was despite some of the inmates having been there for more than fifty years. And he had been there fewer than eight.

Of course, he'd had an unfair advantage when it came to earning the guards' trust. He'd committed only one crime in his life. He'd shot his divorce lawyer with a sawed-off shotgun. Don't get me wrong, I have nothing against divorce lawyers. However, I would point out that the divorce rate among prison guards at the time was reputed to be above 75 percent. Apparently, a lot of them thought Bill a hero.

His status as an otherwise law-abiding citizen, and the fact that he was reputed to be the smartest inmate in the prison, and the fact he was White, all led Bill to be elevated to assistant to the prison chaplain, assistant to the deputy superintendent, assistant to the head of the canine unit, and note taker for the early morning meetings during which White officers would scheme and plot about how to rig promotions for the White guards.

But this was his boldest scheme yet. The Mississippi Department of Corrections was under strict orders from the governor not to corroborate a thing. And yet Bill had figured out how to deliver one of the top leaders of the prison as my other source. I knew that they would claim it had all been fabricated if they could. I had to figure out how to get the recording without him knowing.

I went to the local Radio Shack and was introduced to a simple $4.99 device with a suction cup on a microphone. The guy at the counter said, "Plug this into your tape recorder. Lick that, stick it to the top of the phone, not the bottom, and you'll capture the whole conversation, but it's got to be close to the earpiece to hear what they're saying." With that, we were off to the races.

Turns out, I didn't know any White Southern Belles in Mississippi. The place was intensely segregated. And then it hit me. There was a new head of the Mississippi ACLU, and she was White. And they said she was born and raised in Hattiesburg. I gave her a call. She was totally down. Conversation after conversation, week after week for three weeks, the prison official Bill had recommended corroborated his reports.

The fourth week we called him again, but he could not be found, not anywhere. It was as if he had been "disappeared," but that was all right with us. We had three weeks' worth on the record. Our story was corroborated. And with that, the FBI began to be responsive. Bill was transferred. I went up to see him at the Lafayette County Jail, where he was being held briefly while awaiting transport to a federal prison out of state.

When I saw Bill, he gave me a hero's welcome. And I gave him the same. I asked him, "Why did you do it, Bill? Did you know Freddy?" Freddy was the Black inmate who was found murdered and buried in the shallow grave.

"No, I never met him. But I'll tell you this. As far as I'm concerned, Freddy was my brother. If they could do that to him, then they could do it to any of us."

It was a simple statement of solidarity, given the history of Parchman, truly the last antebellum plantation in the state of Mississippi. It was also the closest I'd ever come to hearing a White indentured servant express why he would fight alongside a Black slave.

Editor's note: Our paper, the *Jackson Advocate*, was firebombed again. It was 1998. I was a student at Oxford then. I called Mr. Tisdale immediately and asked, "Was it the Klan like last time?"

"No," he shot back decisively.

"Why are you so certain?" I inquired.

"Well, as you might recall, I started taking the leading local White supremacist to lunch after they shot us up and burned us down last time."

I'd forgotten about that. Almost reflexively. He was talking about the notorious White nationalist Richard Barrett.

"Anyway, we have kept at it. We both love debating possible alternative outcomes to the Civil War, and no one else in town wants to debate either one of us, so we just keep debating each other.

"Barrett called me this morning," he continued, "he wanted to make sure I knew it wasn't any of his people. We both agreed that the most likely suspects are a certain set of local business leaders—including an Uncle Tom—who hate that our paper complains about their discriminatory redevelopment schemes and are betting everyone else will just assume it's the Klan again."

Apparently, even a life-long White supremacist can get tired of being exploited by those who profit by pitting groups against each other.

The last time I saw Richard Barrett he came to say his last respects as Mr. Tisdale lay dying in a bed at the local Veteran's Administration hospital. He asked for a moment of privacy. I gave him my seat at my dying publisher's bedside and stepped out of the room.

Through the cracked door, I heard the man who for decades had been reputed to be the local Grand Wizard of the Ku Klux Klan start to sob. I drew closer to the door. I heard him begin to pray. He said, "God please save and protect his soul. Lord, this man listened to me, this man understood me, this man was my friend."

I could not help but wonder what might have happened if they had started having those lunches decades earlier.

17

THE FIRST STATE SOUTH
OF THE MASON-DIXON

In March 2013, I took a seat in the balcony viewing area of the Maryland State Senate chambers. I was sitting next to Kirk Bloodsworth. By then he was an old friend. I had met him almost two decades earlier when I was serving as the director of the National Coalition to Abolish the Death Penalty.

I knew Kirk's story well. He was a White working-class guy who had been sent to death row as an innocent man. Kirk was a former active-duty marine and waterman on the Eastern Shore of Maryland. In 1985, he was wrongly convicted of murder, and spent nine years in prison, two of those on death row. When DNA testing became available and proved his innocence, he was pardoned.

Kirk was well aware he was part of the biggest demographic on death row: the working poor. On average, 95 percent of our nation's death row inmates did not have enough money to hire a defense lawyer.[1] That was true for Kirk on the day he was arrested as it was throughout his sham of a trial at the hand of one of Maryland's most notoriously ambitious and corrupt prosecutors.

This night was different. We were in the state capitol with hope that the vote would go our way, and that finally, Frederick Douglass's home state would abolish the death penalty. It was close. We were counting every vote, and suddenly, we realized we had won.

I breathed a sigh of relief. Abolishing the death penalty in Maryland was the fulfillment of a promise I had made not just to Kirk, but to another death row inmate, Troy Davis, an innocent man executed in Georgia two years earlier. Troy had insisted that we do more to publicize his case, to help the public understand the utterly inhuman nature of fallible humans executing their peers.

It worked. Awareness of his case drove support for the death penalty to an all-time low across the country. This had made it possible for us to abolish the death penalty in Connecticut a year earlier, even though there was a high-profile case involving the murder of an heiress in the headlines at the same time.

I was also relieved because in a significant way we were finishing a race Frederick Douglass had started long ago. Douglass was the first civil rights leader to publicly call for the abolition of the death penalty. He said that its roots were intertwined with those of the lynching tree, and that both must be cut down and destroyed.

Finally, abolishing the death penalty in Maryland was also the culmination of a bold strategy that young activists throughout the state had insisted we pursue.

A year earlier, our coalition met to discuss our multiple strategies to advance civil rights in Maryland. In addition to abolishing the death penalty, civil rights leaders had big ambitions that year for advancing immigrant rights and LGBT equality. The NAACP had stepped in to lead the final push. I had also been asked to co-chair the campaign to pass the DREAM Act in the state. Then the newly minted president of the Human Rights Campaign, Chad Griffin, reached out to ask for my thoughts about a campaign to secure marriage equality. I told him I thought we could win. He asked me if I could help. I said, "Of course." I recruited a young organizer from Baltimore named Fagan Harris to help.

At that strategy meeting, I laid out our ambitions. Somebody asked me, "What do the Mikes say?" At the time, the Mikes were the men who ruled Annapolis. Mike Miller was the president of the State Senate. And Mike Busch was the Speaker of the Maryland House of Delegates. I told them that Mike Miller had made it clear he was going to do little if anything to help advance any of our goals. The second Mike said that, given Mike Miller's intransigence, it might be too much to expect to get any of them done.

Fagan looked at me and said, "I guess they might be right. But something just doesn't add up. If we don't pursue the DREAM Act, we're going to demotivate CASA and many other groups from helping to push our entire agenda. If we don't pursue abolishing the death penalty, we'll demoralize the Black community in the larger fight. And if we pull back on marriage equality, we're gonna have a whole bunch of gay rights activists and their allies pull back as well. We simply can't make progress through subtraction and division. So, why don't we just take a deep breath and try a new kind of math they taught us Millennials when we were young. It's called addition and multiplication." He smirked. I smiled and laughed. I knew he was right.

Fagan was a brilliant strategist. In Baltimore, we were proud that there were four Black men who were Rhodes scholars. He was now the fifth. And he had stayed home from Oxford University for the spring in order to help us win these victories. How could I refuse such simple logic? And how could I not respect the fact that so many people were giving up a lot more than even Fagan to help us win?

I said, "All right, Fagan. Let's give it a shot."

Back at NAACP headquarters, some quietly questioned if we were "taking on too much" by pursuing three simultaneous, massive political battles in Maryland. When they did, I would remind them that in addition to giving us our charge to abolish the death penalty, Frederick Douglass's example called on us to be fearless allies as well.

They got quiet and leaned in when I spoke about Douglass. I started by recounting the civil rights architecture the old brick mason turned orator, author, and organizer had helped build for us: the Thirteenth, Fourteenth, and Fifteenth Amendments to the U.S. Constitution. He built the abolitionist movement first as an escaped slave and then as a freedman. The Thirteenth Amendment abolished slavery. The Fourteenth guaranteed equality to all of us and secured birthright citizenship for everyone in this country: for former Confederates, whose citizenship was being challenged because they had taken up arms against their nation's government; for former slaves, whose citizenship was challenged by folks who still thought them subhuman; for children of Chinese railroad workers, who were viciously maligned and abused.

The Fifteenth Amendment guaranteed Black men the right to vote. Well aware that poor White men were only granted the right to vote two decades earlier, when property owning requirements were eliminated and with taxpaying requirements disenfranchising poor White men in at least five states as recently as 1860, Douglass was eager to see the nation's promise of one America, one vote realized for everyone.

After recounting Douglass's seminal victories as an abolitionist, I laid out his bold actions as an ally to the equality struggle of women and immigrants of color. White supremacist conservatives in the U.S. Senate responded to the passage of the Fourteenth Amendment by introducing the Chinese Exclusion Act. Douglass responded to them by crusading against it, championing the humanity of Chinese American immigrants and the utter strength of our nation, and clowning the cowardice of anyone who feared immigrants who weren't European. Black people celebrated the Fifteenth Amendment, Black men signed up to vote, and many, like my mom's great-grandfather Peter G. Morgan, declared their campaigns. But Douglass did something very different, I explained to my colleagues: he announced he would *not* cast a vote until women had the right to vote too.

Then I explained that the struggle for marriage equality had touched his life too. After he was widowed, he married a White woman. They lived safely together in Washington, D.C., well aware that he could be lynched for his marriage just one inch outside the city boundary in any direction.

The press interrogated him about having a White wife. He replied to a reporter's question on the matter only once. The widower stated the obvious, "My first wife was the color of my mother. My second wife is the color of my father." With that, he dropped the proverbial mic and moved on.

To the naysayers who accused us of doing too much, I would close by saying, "Fighting for immigrants' rights was right then. It's right now, too. The battle for marriage equality was right then. The battle for marriage equality was right when my parents fought it. The battle for marriage equality is right now, too."

By embracing the math of addition and multiplication, everyone started to pull in the same direction. The man who led that effort was Travis Tazelaar. He embraced the intersectional strategy fully and blanketed the state with signs that said simply, "Pass the DREAM Act. Pass marriage equality. Abolish the death penalty." With our victory over the death penalty in the Maryland Senate, we won everything we set out to win that legislative year. The next year, those victories needed to be ratified on the ballot by popular referendum. We knew Miller and his allies might try something to help the conservatives defeat us at the ballot box. We were confident we could win there, too.

When all was said and done, we made Maryland the first state in the South to do any of those things—and the first state in the nation to do all of them.

Still, when the dust settled and the last toast was made at the last celebration, after we passed landmark civil rights legislation, expanded voting rights, and passed sensible gun safety reform, I looked around the room and couldn't help but feel uneasy that there was no other working-class White guy in the room except for Kirk Bloodsworth.

Suddenly a memory came flooding back to me. I was walking with an old organizer turned foundation president named Kirke Wilson. We were talking about how we might win bigger victories for working families. He paused, and said, "Never forget, Ben, when the table of leadership meets in the movement, there's no one who speaks for the poor White Protestant man who's not a union member. And there is a lot of them."

Kirke's point was that while we might be able to win civil rights victories without them in the room, those victories will remain fragile, and winning major victories against poverty—victories like those FDR won when he passed the New Deal—will be almost impossible until we rebuild the old bridge between the two groups.

Fagan's math was the answer. We just had to expand the equation and build a larger, more resiliant brotherhood and sisterhood. We do that and we might actually be on our way to healing our nation and ending the legacy of race and racism. If we neglect that responsibility, we all do so at our own peril.

18

A RACE WAR
BEGINS AND ENDS

It was seven thirty a.m. on a Monday in the middle of March 2012. I got a call on my cell phone. It was the president of the Florida NAACP, Adora Obi Nweze. From the tone of her voice, she was clearly in a panic. "I need you down here right away," she started. "I'm afraid a race war is about to break out."

I paused for a moment to let her take a deep breath. "What's going on?"

President Obi Nweze was a seasoned leader with a long track record—in her long tenure with the Florida NAACP she had spearheaded several lawsuits against the state and been appointed to several state commissions. She was always a steady leader, but I could feel the tension in her voice this morning.

She went right into it. "Well, at five o'clock this morning, two of our local chapter members, daycare workers, were at McDonald's on their way to work. Out of nowhere, a White supremacist jumped into the back of their car and started slapping them in the back of the head, screaming, over and over, 'I know what you Black bitches are trying to do.' Some of the McDonald's employees chased the man away. But I'm worried, Ben, this place is a tinderbox."

"Slow down," I interrupted, "Back up a second; what's going on?

Why is a White supremacist jumping into the back of someone's car at a McDonald's?"

"Ben, it has been weeks now since that boy was killed up in Sanford, Florida," she continued, "and we've been campaigning to get the self-appointed neighborhood watchman who shot and killed him arrested. Since then, the situation has gotten out of hand. White supremacists have come to town, patrolling the streets, saying that they are there to protect the White citizens. Black nationalists have shown up in town saying that they are there to protect the Black citizens. We need to get them all out of town, and we need to get the locals organized so that the town can heal itself.

"But it's getting worse by the day," she went on, "The local police aren't helping matters either. This is the second time in two years that a Black person has been wrongfully killed in that town. And yet again they refuse to do anything. The last time, it was a Black homeless man who was hit upside the head by a boy playing an internet-inspired game called One Punch. He sucker-punched the man right in his skull and killed him. Later on, it was discovered that the boy was related to a police officer. He was never punished. It's a mess, Ben. I need your help. And I need you here today because we have a mass meeting tonight and I'm worried, Ben, I'm worried that a riot could break out before we even get to the meeting."

I took a deep breath.

It was Monday. I had just told my wife that I was going to be home all week, a rare treat for any national president of the NAACP. I traveled more than two hundred days a year, responding to crises like this, helping to build our membership, speaking at local dinners to raise money for the organization. And yet I could hear in the voice of one of our wisest, most cool-headed state presidents that I needed to get on the next plane to Florida. I turned my truck around and returned home.

I took a moment to explain to my wife that I would need to go to Florida as quickly as possible. The look in her eye killed me. She was a seasoned civil rights lawyer who understood the urgency. She was also a wife, a mother, and four months pregnant with our second child. We both had been looking forward to me being home. After all, we needed to be together, our daughter wanted her daddy home, and I needed to take care of more than a few things in order to prepare for the baby's arrival.

Sure, other men might wait longer to prepare the nursery, but when your life is a constant drumbeat of crisis response, you learn to plan in advance. Losing that week was going to set me back. I promised her I would get back as fast as I could.

When I landed in Orlando, a small team of local volunteers met me and rushed me to Sanford. We arrived at Allen Chapel AME Church in the Goldsboro neighborhood.

A century ago, Goldsboro was its own town, a free Black town like Rosewood. A place created originally as a safe harbor for former slaves. Since then, it had been forcibly incorporated into Sanford, and yet never actually felt like a part of the town.

Tonight, the church where the mass meeting was being held was overflowing. There were approximately a thousand people inside and three thousand outside. The police monitoring the situation never left their patrol cars. They occasionally raced back and forth, apparently trying to keep the streets clear, given the overflowing crowd on the church lawn. I have dealt with tense situations in almost every region of the country, but this was the most unrestrained and unprofessional display of police power I had ever seen, anywhere. I went inside, stood at the back of the room, and listened. The pastor beckoned me to the front.

I greeted the crowd and asked them about their experiences. It was clear they were worried about the need to charge young Trayvon Martin's killer, and yet they were probably even more worried about what his not being charged meant for each of their own lives. A man raised his hand. I asked him what was on his mind.

"Down here, our lives are worth less than a dog," he started. "A man shot a dog in Sanford not too long ago. They sentenced him to two years. Once again, someone's killed one of us. Once again, the police ain't doing nothing about it."

The room erupted with agreement and anger. Kevin Myles, our southeast regional director, stepped up and whispered in my ear that the crowd outside had begun marching toward the police station.

"Make sure we send our volunteers to march with them," I said. "Keep it under control."

"One step ahead of you, boss," he responded. "We have the DOJ community relations service working with us. We're all embedded in the crowd. We got it handled." I was confident that he was right. The volunteers of the Seminole County NAACP and the Florida State Conference NAACP were top notch. The DOJ Community Relations team was led by my fraternity brother Thomas Battle. He was a true professional and deeply committed to being a peacekeeper in every way.

I went back to listening to people's stories. One by one, town members stepped forward to recount instances of being humiliated and abused by local police officers. Hours passed. When it crossed midnight, I said to the crowd, "We all need to get a good night's sleep. It's clear there's a lot more to be said. If anybody has not had a chance to speak tonight, I will meet you here tomorrow at noon. I'll bring NAACP national staff with me and we will take down your stories and get them to the DOJ so they can bring a 'pattern-and-practice' investigation."

The mood shifted in the room, and with that, the crowd dispersed.

When I arrived back at noon the next day, the room was packed. Scores of people were waiting to be called as witnesses, and at least sixteen news agencies were ready to cover it. Every local station had a camera there. Most national networks did too. Some international networks as well.

I brought our "national staff" with me. It was a young man named Ben Wrobel. The two of us started to panic. It occurred to me that I was about to preside over the most recorded and televised civil rights hearing of which I had ever been a part, and we had not vetted a single witness. Our movement has always been disciplined to a fault, making sure that when people get in front of the microphone to talk about perceived atrocities and injustices, we are actually hearing from people who have experienced atrocities and injustices. If I got the right crackpot on the mic or a few in a row, it could discredit everything. I looked at the crowd slowly face by face.

I decided to give it a shot. They all looked credible, and the fact they had all stayed there late and showed up early was not insignificant. One by one people came forward and recounted their tales. One man stood up and told us about getting pulled over on the side of the highway and getting harassed by a local police officer without cause. Another woman told us how one officer regularly pulled her over, to the point that she got to know the officer by name. Several young men around Trayvon Martin's age came up and shared their own experiences of harassment by the Sanford police.

Every story told that day appeared credible, legitimate, and legitimately concerning. Every witness to the hearings listened with rapt attention. My researchers sent the notes back to the NAACP national office, which sent them on to the U.S. Department of Justice (DOJ). The mayor's staff was in the room taking notes, as was somebody from the city manager's office. The hearing lasted over four hours.

Most important, the Black residents of Sanford who spoke felt heard.

Afterward, I went to meet with pastors who were organizing to pull the town together, along with the local head of the NAACP, Turner Clayton, Jr.

President Clayton had spent the last quarter century as either a member of local law enforcement or as local head of the NAACP. For about eight of those years, he had both roles. His fear that something like this could happen had driven him to become a civil rights activist while working as a member of law enforcement. The fact that he had played both roles made him invaluable in this moment.

The mayor, Jeff Triplett, was a White Republican who had been in office for a year. The city manager, Norton N. Bonaparte, Jr., was a Black Democrat who had been in his position less than seven months. Both were overwhelmed. The city manager was clearly dealing with more drama than he'd expected to encounter in his first year in office. Mayor Triplett confessed he had run for office thinking it would be a part-time job. Sanford City Hall is open only a few days a week, and Triplett ran a successful local company. He'd never expected to manage a 24/7 crisis like this.

It was clear the mayor had been moved by media and staff retelling of the reports at Allen Chapel Church that surfaced the day before. He was ready to truly hear the people of Goldsboro talk about their pain, perhaps for the first time.

The mayor and the city manager were clearly working as a team now, and they were grateful for the guidance of our local NAACP president. His status as both a retired member of the local law enforcement community and an esteemed civil rights leader counted for a lot. After all, his tenure serving their community was almost twenty times that of the two of them put together. We all turned to him and asked what he thought we should do.

His response was simple: "Get rid of the police chief." Not only had both of these killings happened on his watch but before he was police chief he was head of the police academy. If there were improperly trained police officers on this force, he was the one who trained them. If there were police officers being led in the wrong direction, he was the one leading them.

The room fell quiet. All eyes shifted back to the mayor. The mayor agreed with his assessment.

In a matter of weeks, the police chief was replaced and a new chief installed. This chief listened to Goldsboro—and the entire city of Sanford—and swift changes followed.

One of the initiatives that the chief introduced was deceptively simple. Every Thursday morning, the new chief required every single police officer to stop whatever they were doing, get out of their patrol car, and hand out business cards to everyone they encountered for the course of one hour.

In the wealthier and Whiter parts of town, such concierge service was expected. In communities like Goldsboro, it was a shock. It confused people. And ultimately, it was a relief. Many citizens in Goldsboro believed that finally, the police officers were there to keep them safe, too.

That work, that listening, that empathy, that mutual self-discovery and reckoning that happened in Sanford pulled the city together. It didn't create a utopia; it didn't make things perfect; but it did improve the situation more rapidly than anybody thought possible.

A little more than a year later, I was back down in Florida for the NAACP national convention in Orlando. We had planned the location years before; but as fate would have it, our convention was being held the same week as the expected verdict in case of the killer of Trayvon Martin, being held in a courthouse just a few miles away.

We planned for every contingency. We worked with local and national authorities to make sure that if the verdict went the wrong way, the risk to human life and property would be minimized in every possible way.

As Saturday night arrived, we noted that the verdict hadn't come down yet. Some hoped it might not come until Monday. But at eleven p.m., I got a call that the judge would deliver the verdict imminently.

"Really?" I queried the caller. "What is the judge thinking? Eleven o'clock on a Saturday night: the hour of maximum drunkenness in most places in America. Dropping a racially charged verdict at this hour is like dropping a match next to a gallon of gasoline."

I hung up the call and turned on the news.

The killer was acquitted on every charge. Cheers erupted from White citizens across the city. I could hear them in my hotel room, the rumble of applause. In an eerie coincidence, 11 p.m. was also the hour fireworks went off at the local amusement parks.

The cacophony from shouts of joy made me shudder. I picked up my baby boy from his crib and cried. I knew that we were prepared for this moment and our staff was executing our plans. The DOJ was executing its plans. But I worried about Orlando. I thought about the same White supremacists in Sanford from a year and a half earlier. They were there now most likely creating more problems for innocent bystanders. I thought about the ultra-Black nationalists as well, and their response to the verdict.

I worried about a lot of cities that night. Our theory was simple: The best way to avoid violence was to give the people a constructive way to help get justice. We quickly sent out emails assuring activists across the country there was still hope. We asked them to help us call on the U.S. Department of Justice to bring federal civil rights charges against the killer. White supremacist hackers attacked our servers. We pushed out the same message by text. Our mobile list exploded as hundreds of thousands of Americans used their cell phones to answer our call.

I handed my son to his mom and went downstairs to address the assembled leaders of the NAACP Youth and College divisions. As I looked into their eyes, my heart broke. They were all more or less the age of Trayvon Martin. They had grown up knowing the police could kill them and get away with it. Now, apparently, a self-appointed neighborhood watch guy could do the same thing. My comments were compassionate, brief, and focused on our call for the DOJ to take action.

I invited them to step up and share their thoughts.

As they did, my heart swelled with pride. Helping to win justice and heal our nation was always tough work, but they were clearly more than up to the challenge. For the past five years we had all worked together to revive the NAACP's old tradition of fighting for justice for individual Black women, men, and children who were being mistreated by our justice system. From Georgia to Mississippi to Florida we had crisscrossed the Deep South with campaigns fighting to free the wrongfully incarcerated and to win justice for the loved ones of those wrongfully killed. We had won some; we had lost some. Throughout the process we had built a bigger movement and developed young leaders who were now poised to win great victories of their own.

The one city I did not worry about was Sanford, Florida. The place where the killing had occurred. In the eighteen months since I had first touched down there, I watched the city listen across old lines of division. Whites listened to Blacks. Police listened to people who they previously regarded only as a nuisance. Black pastors listened to police officers. Black residents listened to police officers. Business cards and numbers were exchanged. Tips were made. Trust was built because respect had been given.

It all had started with listening. Listening is the most transformative sign of respect we show our fellow human beings.

19

AN AMERICAN PARABLE

Stacey Abrams slipped into a pew two rows behind mine. She handed my daughter Morgan a DVD player, two movies, and a set of headphones. She was known throughout the state as a rising star in Georgia politics. To my daughter, she was simply Aunt Stacey. And to me, she was a friend who always had a little bit more common sense than I had.

I'm a fifth-generation member of the NAACP. Children in my family have always been raised with the hard truths about our national sickness of racism. Still, Stacey understood, well before I did, that the hard truths to be aired in the church that day would be too much for any seven-year-old child to bear.

Two rows in front of me, a man was coming undone as he retold the story. More than a half century earlier he was a child not that much older than Morgan was then. His uncles returned from a night out with hundreds of other men. They had killed "four niggers" that night. Well, actually five: two couples, and a baby they cut from one woman's belly— a baby he said that his father and uncles believed was the child of one of their fellow Klansmen.

The Moore's Ford Bridge lynching is notorious in Georgia to this day. It was the last of Georgia's lynch mob incidents, and was among the most gruesome ever recorded. The Klan typically only lynched men and raped women; killing a woman and her unborn child was beyond the pale, even for them.

I was relieved that Morgan's ears were shielded by large headphones booming Eddie Murphy's "Nutty Professor" into her little brain. I needed to ask some questions. We needed every last detail.

I may have been the national president of the NAACP, but in that moment, I was back in investigative reporter mode. I was recording the man on my iPad as he spoke. I had instructions to send the file directly to the DOJ as soon as we were done.

The lynching had been unsolved for too long. This man, as a boy, had witnessed the unspeakable; now he was recounting in the moment what had happened. The memories were burned into his brain, the same way memories of the woman scarred by the curling iron had been seared into mine so many years earlier. However, this quintuple homicide was magnitudes greater and cut much deeper. Hate that violent leaves an indelible mark on the soul of all who come near it.

This witness had asked for us to come and listen to him. After many decades holding poison inside, he needed to let it out. As the facts gushed out, you could see him shake as if his own soul were beginning to implode. And then, just like that, all the facts were out. He breathed a sigh of relief, stood up a little straighter, and walked out of the church looking a lot lighter than he had when he walked in. I can only liken it to witnessing an exorcism.

Looking around, it was clear that few of us were prepared for what we had heard—the details, the braggadocio, the lack of remorse among the killers. The way the man shivered as the facts came out of him. The way you could see the broken heart of a little boy who had revered the men in his life until that moment—and then had to live with them for decades after, knowing that they were capable of being the most vicious monsters.

As I walked out of the church, I was reminded that his experience was not unique. My thoughts drifted back to a story I once heard from a hero of mine, a man who, like this witness, had been born the son of a Klansman. His name was Bob Zellner. He went on to become one of the founders of the Student Nonviolent Coordinating Committee. He shared a story with me one night before a rally organized by Reverend Dr. William Barber in North Carolina.

Years later, he put that story down on paper in a letter to my mother. It is captured in her book *Combined Destinies*. Along with her co-author, Carolyn Haskell, also a trained therapist, my mom compiled the stories of fifty-two White people whose lives have been indelibly harmed by the racism directed at Black people.

If that fact seems impossible, consider what that might say about how racism has impacted your own life. As the title suggests, their book, like the story I heard in the church, and the one I heard that night from Bob, all gave testimony to the indisputable truth Dr. King observed: "We are all bound together in a single garment of destiny."

Here's the letter Bob Zellner wrote to my mom. I offer it as a unique document worth reading in full:

Dear Ann,

When I was asked to write about how race discrimination has damaged white people, my mind was forced to shift gears. We usually confine our thinking to how racism has harmed those it is directed against, and I had never thought about the ways in which I was harmed. In reflecting on my assignment, however, I am realizing that racial hatred's persistent, deep stain on our present and past has hurt us all.

I grew up in south Alabama, the cradle of the American Bible Belt, where children were to be seen, not heard. We lived in or own little world, separate from adults for the most part, except for the occasional housekeeper or babysitter. Talk of race, religion, philosophy, or politics was out of earshot of little people because, Grandma Hardy said, "Little pitchers have big ears." Such secrecy was scary, causing me to feel vulnerable and insecure. The notion that there were things on this earth that even Mom and Dad had no power over made me afraid. Infidelity, violence, scandals, and such were discussed, if at all, in hushed voices—not openly like today.

Our own family scandal was Daddy's "nervous breakdown." I don't remember how my brothers reacted to Dad's malady, but insecurity and dread caused my intestines to telescope, according to the local doctor. That psychosomatic condition caused me intense abdominal pain. Southern families have always been famous for the eccentric bachelor uncle or maiden aunt locked in the attic wearing only Confederate gray or antebellum gowns. Mental disorder was scandalous and something to be ashamed of. Southern writers have mined this trove for decades. . . .

Dad's participation and membership in the Ku Klux Klan (KKK) was, without doubt, a primary cause of his breakdown. You can't be a minister of the gospel and practice racial hatred without paying a significant psychological price. Although the Klan connection was never mentioned, Dad's dilemma, like the American one, was preaching one thing about race while doing another. Having half the population lording over the other half, taking the best of everything while leaving the rest to make do on scraps, was bad enough. But my father had also figured that holding black people down was impoverishing a majority of white people. He began preaching that if you were a poor, working-class white person in the South holding the black man down in the ditch, you should realize that you are down in the ditch with him. A rich man, Dad said, walked down the center of the road laughing at both men in the ditch—the black one and the white one.

Wealthy people, remembering the "patty rollers" of slavery times, were content to let "white trash" do the dirty work. Before the Emancipation Proclamation was signed, common whites, owning no slaves, were often paid by slaveholders to patrol the roads looking for runaway slaves. They were called patty rollers. Ne'er-do-well white folk gained a false pride by having more social status than the "niggers." And the thought, "One never knows, I might just own me some slaves someday."

This is much like today when many poor and working-class white

Southern males of a certain age support the right-wing policies of Republicans dictating low taxes for the richest Americans. "You never know," say these dreamers, "I could be rich someday myself, and I would not like to be taxed."

As little boys, my brothers and I had no idea of racism and its possible connection with my father's sickness. We just knew something was wrong with Daddy, and we wanted him to get better so he could play with us again. I felt abandoned and not worth very much, what with Mom busy teaching and being "the minister's wife" while Daddy was absent a lot. We didn't understand that Dad was undergoing a crisis of conscience.

Dad's family and surroundings had determined his identity, wrapped up to an usual degree in "the race question." Raised in Birmingham, a raw, bustling industrial cauldron, he grew up in a relatively young city unleavened by the noblesse oblige paternalism sometimes found in older Southern metropolises. Young James Abraham Zellner was not exposed to even the tiny liberalizing influences I found during my high school days in Mobile. New Orleans on the Gulf Coast, and cities of the Atlantic seaboard, like Charleston and Savannah, were much more cosmopolitan and relatively sophisticated. Granddaddy Zellner was a telegrapher and later a dispatcher on the GM&O Railroad, a hotbed of Klan activity. He taught his three sons and two daughters to be white supremacists. As the oldest son, my father pleased his father by becoming, after initiation into the secret brotherhood, a Klan organizer, or Kleagle, with responsibility for recruiting new members.

As a child, then, I was injured by the system of apartheid in America. My injury, however, was not as apparent or as immediate as the damage being done to Mom and Dad. Dad, ambitious to do well in the ministry, was torn between advancement professionally on the one hand and his emerging conviction that racial oppression and discrimination were both immoral and un-Christian.

Before I started school, we lived in Newton, Alabama, which was near Dothan, the economic hub of southeast Alabama and parts of the Florida

Panhandle. I have no conscious memory of race ever being discussed or even mentioned, but in later life I had flashes of memory of virulent racism from that time. The memories consist of horrible screams of pain and loud whacks like a whip hitting a telephone pole. When asked about these things Mother said I could be recalling scout initiations. Dad was involved, as were we boys, in scouting. . . .

A pall of shame descended over me when I learned it takes a village—no, an entire region—to raise and maintain a system of economic exploitation based on race and the circumstances of one's birth. Mom and Dad, big on shame and its uses, often chastised us with "Aren't you ashamed of yourself?" delivered in the proper tones of disappointment. This was a feared consequence of even the most minor infraction.

The shame I felt as a white Southerner, however, that my people had systematically injured and beaten down a whole other people, was exponentially worse and of greater magnitude than small shames, like the time I was caught playing "doctor" with Linda Barnhill, a parishioner's daughter.

My feelings of shame changed to an aching guilt that I had benefited from the misery of others. As a young teenager, I had tried to imagine how black boys my age could deal with their rage toward white bullies. My only fear in dealing with bullies was that they would beat me up unless I was successful in beating them. Young black men, feeling their manhood, were told by their elders not to fight back because it might cost them their lives. White men might kill them for being uppity, or they might disappear into the prison archipelago stretching across the South. Prison labor was such that businesses and plantations bought and sold convicts just like in the old days of slavery.

While researching and writing *The Wrong Side of Murder Cree: A White Southerner in the Freedom Movement*, a memoir of my experiences as an adult in the civil rights movement, I could not avoid asking why so few white Southerners took part in the front lines of the struggle that came to be known as the Second American Civil War. Why did white Southerners leave the heavy lifting to our black brothers and sisters and their Northern allies? Why were the overwhelming majority of Germans "good Germans" during the Holocaust? One day I tried to think of a white Southern slaveholder who, at the height of his or her power, wealth, and political influence, freed his slaves to become an active abolitionist. I confess I could not find a single one.

Answering my own question, I reasoned that during slavery, whites across the nation, especially the South, maintained that institution through force, violence, and terror. To enslave a fellow human being is an act of war against that person. In order to wage war against a person or a people, it becomes necessary to learn to hate that person, "those people."

In order to own a human, as opposed to say, a mule, the owner or slaveholder must deny the humanity of that man, woman, or child. So, growing up in south Alabama among a people who had, for centuries, practiced treating people like objects or mules, I was expected to do likewise. In order to accomplish this degree of dehumanization, the ruling race suffers a shriveling of its own soul and spirit. Over time, farm children, trying to get over their tender-heartedness when killing chickens, rabbits, pigs, and other livestock, manage to harden their hearts. In the same way, many Southerners get over their innate dislike of mistreating others. They teach themselves and their children, "Blacks aren't the same as you and I, and so it is okay to mistreat them."

Eventually, in an effort to gain understanding of my memory flashes of childhood, I looked up racial incidents that occurred in southeast Alabama when I was little. Maybe, I thought, something happened before I was born that people were still talking about. Perhaps there was something so horrible that it still lives in the unconscious of the people of Alabama and northwest Florida.

I came across the following, which could explain my earliest memories of the problems of race and the South. I will condense and paraphrase to remove some of the horror surrounding the death of a twenty-three-year-old black man in south Alabama, just before I was born. Walter White, the courageous anti-lynching NAACP investigator, uncovered this horrific story while launching a national campaign against lynching.

On October 19, 1934, Claude Neal, a twenty-three-year-old peanut farmer, was arrested for the murder of Lola Cannidy, twenty. After confessing under torture, Neal was moved to a jailhouse twenty miles away, supposedly for safekeeping: the lynching spirit in the region was high. But in the middle of the night of October 26 he was removed from the jail by lynch mobs, driven about two hundred miles, and dumped on the road in front of the Cannidy home. Neal was tortured for ten or twelve hours.

Railroad companies in several Southern states laid on special trains, transporting thousands to the scene of the "lynching party" in southeast Alabama. The owners, happy to turn a profit, may have felt like ticket sellers at the Roman Coliseum, where Christians were fed to lions, but that feeling is not recorded in the NAACP records. Needless to say, merchants in and near my hometown must have had a field day supplying thousands of members with rope, food, and drink.

Neal's body was tied to a rope on the rear of an automobile and dragged over the highway to the Cannidy home. Here, a mob estimated to number somewhere between 3,000 and 7,000 people from eleven Southern states was excited awaiting his arrival. When the car dragging Neal's body came to the Cannidy home, a man who was riding the rear bumper cut the rope.

A woman came out of the Cannidy house and drove a butcher knife into his heart. Then the crowd came by, kicking him; some drove their cars over him.

Little children who lived in the neighborhood waited with sharpened sticks for the return of Neal's body and, when it rolled in the dust on the road that awful night, these little children drove their weapons deep into the flesh of the dead man.

Later, Claude Neal's body was hung high in the town square, casting a long shadow over the seething crowd. In addition to being a possible explanation for my earliest memories of the problems of race and the

South, the grisly case of Claude Neal illustrates the emotional and spiritual damage that racism and its practices have inflicted upon my family and home.

Imagine an entire region of people who mistreated black people, a mild and profoundly understated way of describing the terrible institution of slavery, from 1617 to 1865, a period of more than two hundred years. Now, think of the same people re-enslaving black people under Jim Crow and the sharecropper and prisoners-for-purchase systems for the hundred years leading up to 1965.

If you can imagine growing up in such a region, you will have some understanding of what I experienced. That was the region of my childhood and adolescence and those were the people—friends, fellow church members, family, and acquaintances—I grew up around. They were people so steeped in racism and self-hatred that nothing was as it seemed to be.

Would not such people have shriveled hearts? Small hearts don't have room for the milk of human kindness. It is difficult for me to believe that these are the people I grew up with and looked up to. Has human kindness dried up in Southern white people?

Is this why the South today constitutes a lowland where acidic puddles of racist poison stagnate, especially among the older population? Only 10 percent of white people who voted in Alabama pulled the lever for our first black president, Barack Obama. White Southerners still call him "the foreigner," thus rejecting the legitimacy of a black president.

How different is it today from the time that Claude Neal was the forty-fifth lynching since FDR entered the White House on March 4, 1933?

My father and mother came a long way from their upbringing in the segregated South, and they suffered as a result of racism. However, our family has a happy ending dealing with race and its wounds. Quitting the Klan, my father was not content to be an average Southerner and hew to the middle of the road on race and its hurtful consequences. He had been an activist as a Klansman, and he became an activist in the civil rights movement. Working with Rev. Joseph Lowery in Mobile, where I graduated from high school, he participated in the peaceful integration of public buses and became a colleague and behind-the-scenes worker with Dr. Martin Luther King.

I have always been grateful that my parents traveled the long hard road to racial equality and did not teach me to hate people who are different from me. Unlike many of my peers in the South, I was spared taking in the poison of racial hate along with my mother's milk.

As an activist on the front lines of the struggle, I have learned that brotherhood and sisterhood are not so wild a dream as those who profit by postponing it pretend.[1]

When you listen to the child of a Klansman tell you their private story about how the lynchings impacted them—let alone their father— Dr. King's wisdom that our destinies are all connected becomes undeniable. There is no way for you to oppress me and mine without you hurting you and yours. But that's only the half of it.

As I have said, racism is a lie based on a lie.

However, there is another lie. That lie is that racism doesn't hurt White people directly. We have already discussed some of the ways racism against Blacks has hurt White people as individuals. The truth is that racism hurts millions upon millions of White people en masse. How so, exactly? Racism so colors our nation's collective imagination that it renders entire classes of suffering White people virtually invisible. The narratives about Jim Crow barely mention that the era's state-based voter suppression laws also disenfranchised half the White voters in states like Virginia.

During the height of the War on Drugs, in the late 1980s and early 1990s, television news convinced the nation that the biggest group of crack addicts was low-income Black people. It was actually middle-income White people. The news today rarely shows you a photo of a White person in poverty, despite the fact that there are almost twice as many Whites in poverty as Blacks. Ask almost any American what group is dying most frequently from bullets and how, and they will answer, "young Black men from homicide." The actual answer is old White men from suicide.

When I mentioned those suicide rates to a White friend who hosts a podcast, he opened up about six White male friends and family members who had killed themselves, including his dad. He had never spoken about these dead loved ones on air before. Why not? It's not "news." It's time we start talking about the universality of poverty, addiction, and handgun deaths in American communities.

This failure to recognize that large-scale suffering in White communities can ultimately leave people feeling so isolated that they don't realize what's happening to them is part of a much bigger trend.

When those trends are exposed for everyone to see in full view, big changes can happen suddenly. The visibility of White poverty during the Great Depression helped fuel national sentiment to create public jobs programs that employed large numbers of Americans of every color. Most recently, the decision by some sheriffs to start showing the pictures of young White people dying from opiate overdoses helped shift the public conversation about heroin being a crime that needed to be punished to an addiction that needed to be treated. It also made it easier to get the millions of American families who had been suffering silently in the shadows to demand policy solutions that would help their addicted loved ones live better lives.

In short, the legacy of race and racism has led our nation to equate poverty, addiction, and handgun deaths with Black people. In the process, we have ignored even larger numbers of suffering White people and rendered uniting every one of these impacted communities all but impossible. The path to building a better, stronger America starts with being transparent about how many of us—of all colors—are struggling in similar ways.

It would be easy for us to simply blame the media for this problem.

Nonetheless, as the example of those sheriffs reminds us, any group has the power to start correcting it.

The urgency to do so is existential, and not just for Whites. All three of these deep wells of pain converge in any community that has lost a factory. Given that more than 60,000 factories have closed since we passed NAFTA, that's virtually every city and town in our nation. Together, this trifecta of pain—joblessness, drugs, and bullets—has played a significant role in the declining life expectancies of White American men. It is similarly hurting Black American men who used to work, or would have worked, at those same factories. While automation has created additional headwinds that preclude ever returning to manufacturing as we knew it, we will never rebuild the American Dream without first telling the truth about the common struggles of the American people.

20

A HOLLER FROM
THE HOLLERS

N o, no, thank you. Honored, but not interested."
My friend on the other end of the line was disappointed. Larry
Cohen was the outgoing president of the Communication Workers of
America, my union from my days as a journalist in Mississippi. In many
ways, Larry was more than a friend. He was my leader. Through many a
fight, he was right there with a cool head to help me think through how
we could win.

Together, along with the presidents of the Sierra Club and Green-
peace, we founded the Democracy Initiative. It is a multiracial alliance
designed to pull together the voting rights movement and the get-
money-out-of-politics movement. The theory was simple. The voting
rights movement needed more White people to push back against voter
suppression. The get-money-out-of-politics movement needed more
Black folks to push back against corporate lobbyists. I hated saying no
to him. But his request was one I just couldn't wrap my head around.

He wanted me to support Bernie Sanders for president. I knew Bernie
as well as most leaders in the Democratic Party family could claim to,
which is to say, I had met him, I had worked with him, and I respected
him, albeit largely from afar. He was a man of intense integrity and
courage. He also wasn't the easiest person to get to know intimately.

I wanted to say yes. I knew that Bernie, like my father, had been active in the Congress of Racial Equality, when it mattered. He led his college chapter of the Congress of Racial Equality when it merged with SNCC, when it counted. He was arrested, like my father, during CORE's protests when the organization demanded the acceleration of integration. He'd been mistreated by the cops too, just like my father.

Still, I just couldn't bring myself to prioritize his run for president. We all knew what had happened to his fellow Vermonter Howard Dean. Why could Bernie do any better?

Then there was the issue of the Clintons. I had gone all in to help Barack Obama win the 2008 primary. Like most Democrats, at that point, I agreed that 2016 represented Hillary's turn. She wasn't the easiest person to get to know either, but I knew her better than I knew Bernie. Indeed, I volunteered to work as an advance person for both of the Clintons when Bill was president.

Traveling with Bill was wild. I led the advance team for one of his events during his first trip home to Arkansas right after the Monica Lewinsky scandal. The entire advance team was Black, everybody—the men and women organizing the events but also the presidential chefs. Even the Secret Service team, all Black to a one.

That felt intentional. When we walked into a formerly all-White country club to make sure it was prepared just in case the president might decide to play golf while on the weeklong trip, the Black staff scattered at the sight of us barking orders and expressing firm preferences to their White bosses. Then one member of our advance team confessed, "Oh, yeah, my dad's a member here too."

"Too? Why is your father a member of more than one country club in Arkansas?" I asked him, puzzled.

"Well, let's just say that after that dust-up over then Governor Clinton playing at all-White clubs down here in 1992, some were quick to change. Of course, there were many others that didn't. We won't be visiting those today, or ever." I burst out laughing, and then fell quiet.

Bill certainly was pragmatic. He was also incredibly gracious. Our big event was at the home of Truman Arnold. He was as close to a self-made billionaire as I'd ever met. He was the first to pair convenience stores with gas stations, franchised the concept, and called it Roadrunner Markets. It would eventually span the South and Southwest. Like Bill, he was a man of keen intellect and a kind spirit.

We spent six days planning the event at his house. We were told that pretty much anyone who was a friend of Bill's, and owned a jet within four hours of Texarkana, was flying in for it. We spent those six days making sure everything was perfect. And then on the morning of the event, a fast-moving twister came through, knocked over one tent, and left a foot of water in the other.

Standing there, staring at a 30-foot metal pole balanced in a puddle of water a foot deep, I couldn't help but conclude that one stray lightning bolt would transform the entire tent into an execution chamber. Reluctantly, I agreed with the team that we needed to move the event. Fortunately, Truman had just built a multipurpose center at the local community college. There was a basketball game that night, but on account of fact that the president was coming into town, the head of the community college agreed to postpone the game.

We had six hours to move an event for which we prepared for six days. When the president arrived, I was flustered. I never worked so hard or so fast in my life.

I was standing at the door that connected the event room to the parking deck via a secured hallway. As it happened, I was the one who had the key to unlock the deadbolt so that the president could enter the room. All of a sudden, I panicked.

I couldn't find the key.

I searched every pocket. I still couldn't find the key. The Secret Service agent was clearly getting frustrated. Then he leaned close to the door, tapped, and told the president to back away because this boy didn't have the key and he was going to blow off the lock. He started to remove his gun from the holster.

Before he could fire, I looked at him. "I found the key." His eyes said it all: "I should shoot you." I smiled and opened the lock. On the other side of the door was the forty-second president the United States. He greeted us with a smile and said, "Thank you, boys. I needed some time to myself."

And with that, Bill was off to the races, glad-handing, hugging, and kissing the occasional cheek.

A man of incredible grace, he stepped up to the microphone. In between greeting the crowd and starting his prepared remarks, he took a moment to thank the advance team.

I was humbled and honored. Truman was so pleased that the next day he offered to take us out for dinner. He said it was his favorite restaurant. As far as I could tell, it was built in the carcass of an old Cattlemens, a group of steakhouse restaurants in Northern California. You could still see the part of the word that had been covered by the letters of the signage for the Cattlemens chain restaurant on the plywood awning. The sun bleached everything around it, and now it was called something else.

Not to say that it was a bad restaurant. It is to say that there were vinyl checkered tablecloths stapled to picnic tables indoors. I didn't mind it at all. I was just surprised that this restaurant was a billionaire's favorite. Then again, my favorite restaurant is Waffle House—who was I to judge?

Down the middle of our tables were baskets of hors d'oeuvres. The Secret Service arrived just after us and immediately sat down to stuff their faces. The leader of the team was especially hungry. Truman walked over to him and put his hand on his shoulder. "Son, looks like you're enjoying those hors d'oeuvres," Truman observed.

"Yes, sir," the lead agent responded. "What are they?"

"Oh, son," Truman said, bewildered. "You don't know what those are?"

"No, sir."

"Them there are calf fries, son."

"What's a calf fry, sir?" the man slowly responded.

"Calf fries are deep-fried shredded bull balls, son."

The agent stopped chewing. He was quiet. Truman looked bemused. The agent stood up. His complexion turning from mahogany to army green, the agent looked at Truman square in the eye and asked slowly, "Where's the pay phone, sir?"

"Oh, son, I thought you were gonna ask which way is the restroom? Doesn't matter. They're both in the same direction, just walk past the restroom. You'll see the pay phone right there."

"Thank you, sir."

"Why do you want the pay phone son?"

"I need to call my wife, sir. I feel like I just cheated on her."

Truman burst out laughing. We all did.

As I recall, the agent actually walked off to make that phone call. I'm sure they laughed about it all too.

Traveling with Hillary was different. First off, she wasn't the president, she was the First Lady. She had a smaller team. Second, she had an especially ambitious schedule. On what was reportedly her first trip to New York after everyone learned she was planning to run for Senate, our team had a day to plan six events.

She was also more officious than Bill. Her inner team was as well.

Given everything going on back at the White House and the differences in their upbringing, I was more than empathetic. She didn't have Bill's populist touch. But it was clear that deep in her heart she had a concern for the people.

In 2016, as the machine revved up for Hillary's campaign, many activists came to me to say that they were going to support Bernie. They said they just couldn't stomach supporting anyone for president who had once referred to low-income Black children caught up in the criminal justice system as "superpredators." The superpredator theory was pushed by a right-wing criminologist who said that some children were just beyond redemption by the age of six months. That Hillary had pushed it as the former chair of the Children's Defense Fund was unforgivable to many.

I was torn on that point. After all, the 1994 and 1996 crime bills weren't just supported by the likes of Bill Clinton, the Bushes, and Joe Biden. They were also supported by the likes of Maxine Waters and Charlie Rangel. As far as I could tell, each supported them for the same reason: elderly Black voters in the inner cities were demanding them too.

At the time, I was firmly opposed to these bills. I still am. Back then, I felt bewildered and betrayed by the support for bills that were so inhumane and ineffective. Over the years, the dynamic became clearer to me.

When you work in communities full of crime survivors, you ultimately learn that as a group, they will support almost anything you suggest that they think might possibly make them safer. In other words, they will support proposals from the left of the left as well as the right of the right, often simultaneously. If you ask, "Do you want this or do you want that?" the answer will almost certainly be both. Ultimately, they want anything that might just keep them safe.

Still, I was having a hard time endorsing Hillary in the primary. I figured she would win. I was prepared to support her in the general election. I had been through that rodeo many times. After all, I'd started off in politics on the Jesse Jackson campaign and ended up working for the Dukakis campaign.

What stuck with me was the fact that if a primary serves any purpose at all, it's to clarify the issues that the party's standard bearer will hammer home in the general.

Hillary's policy director was my esteemed longtime friend and colleague Maya Harris. Maya, the sister of Kamala Harris, then the California attorney general, was also the former head of the ACLU of

Northern California, and the former number two at the Ford Foundation. She was my grantee in one role and my grantor in another.

We once sat shoulder to shoulder at the Women's Foundation in San Francisco and explained that the principles of feminism sometimes require taking a special interest in men. In short, while incarceration was spiking among Black women, it had been devastatingly high among Black men for decades. Their families were being destroyed. So was a generation of young Black men. Chelsea Clinton would later refer to them as a "missing generation": 1.5 million Black men.

The seeds for that perspective were right there in the Clinton campaign. They were in Maya's hand and I believe they were in Hillary's heart.

When Hillary announced for president, she addressed the need to end mass incarceration head on. Her remorse for her comments twenty years earlier was clear. Yet I had a hard time completely forgiving her. Sometimes I was triggered by her words and would bring them up to others. When folks pushed back to say she had changed, I would eventually concede. After all, she hired Maya; she must have.

Still, I harbored deep concerns about her policy platform, notably her silence on NAFTA.

Before I moved to Mississippi, I worked as a spokesperson against NAFTA for the youth division of the AFL-CIO as well as the Student Environmental Action Coalition. I crisscrossed the country whipping up opposition to NAFTA. Corporate lobbyists said we sounded like Chicken Little.

Two decades and 63,000 closed factories later, every exaggeration that our opposition accused us of making had come true. How could anyone running for president speak to the middle of America without the compassion and courage that Hillary had shown when owning up to her previous position on mass incarceration? How could she not admit that NAFTA was a mistake and clearly call for it to be renegotiated, along with the WTO and every single piece of trade legislation that had betrayed working Americans?

Like Hillary, Bernie said all of the right things on race. What's more, his path to his position was more direct. Some would say that he was less outspoken on race since he had moved to Vermont. Take one look at Vermont and it was obvious to me as to why. Still, no one could take from him the fact that he showed courage when it mattered most in the 1960s when very few White men did, and risked his life for it. Nor could they deny that he had played a leading role in delivering Vermont for both of Jesse Jackson's presidential primary bids, in 1984 and 1988.

Three years later, as the 2016 Democratic Primary revved up in New Hampshire, I replayed my conversation with Larry Cohen from early 2013.

My thoughts drifted back to my favorite uncle. Originally from Maine, he had moved across the border to Bethlehem, New Hampshire, about eighty miles from where his and my dad's parents had grown up in the Granite State hamlet of Lebanon. My uncle Bill is the working-class hero of our family. His older brothers had the privilege of being boys who were raised with a nanny before being sent off to study at great universities. My father was seventeen and their middle brother Jim was fifteen when their father died. Bill, on the other hand, was eight. He felt abandoned by his dad and then triply abandoned when both of his brothers left for college soon after.

From the age of eight, Uncle Bill had to work. After decades as a housewife, Bill's mom, my grandmother, was a young widow and went back to work. Uncle Bill was given a mini tuxedo to wear in order to serve hors d'oeuvres at parties. He had to help pay the bills too.

Uncle Bill always loved me with all his heart and I've always loved him. He is simply one of the best, most genuine people I know. While I was ruminating on who to support in the primary, I realized he had moved across the border to New Hampshire, which was next up in the cycle.

I picked up the phone and called him. I got Aunt Jonnie instead. Uncle Bill was out. She was happy to hear from me but in a hurry. We caught up quickly before I got right to the point.

"Do you know who Bill is supporting in the primary?"

"I don't know," she said impatiently, "but he's torn between Bernie and Trump." I told her I missed her and hung up the phone. (New Hampshire has an "open primary" in which voters can help select the candidate for either party.)

Her answer had alarmed me.

Still, I couldn't criticize Uncle Bill, because I knew his concern was that of millions of working-class men—Black and White—across America. They wagered their entire lives and careers on making stuff. Most worked in factories. Uncle Bill worked in lumberyards. They saw men like Mitt Romney emerge from firms like Bain. They saw women like Hillary Clinton appear from companies like the Rose Law Firm and Walmart. They felt betrayed by both leaders and wanted nothing to do with either of them. In the end, there were only two candidates criticizing NAFTA. One was Bernie and the other was Trump.

I was sure that Uncle Bill was torn. The only real question in his heart was who was going to do more to change the position of men like him?

I had my answer. Now I decided that I needed to have the courage to bring my voice to the race before it was too late. I picked up the phone. I called Larry Cohen and told him I was all in.

The campaign moved quickly to get me involved. They flew a film crew out to Baltimore to record my endorsement. I asked a friend and local social entrepreneur, Chris Wilson, to scout locations and facilitate logistics on the ground.

Chris's story is powerful. He grew up in a tough Washington, D.C., neighborhood at the height of the violent drug trade. He was so afraid for his life that he wouldn't leave the house without a gun. One night, defending himself, he killed a man. At eighteen, he was sentenced to life in prison.

That should have been the end of Chris's story. It wasn't. He ended up writing what he termed his "master plan"—in it he rattled off a list of ambitions and aspirations for his life: learning Italian and Chinese, traveling the world, building a business, starting a family. Behind bars, Chris worked relentlessly to fulfill his master plan. He finished high school, then college. He drafted business plans. He even learned to code by writing out programs, longhand, on yellow notepads.

Nearly twenty years later, the parole judge granted Chris his freedom. She was impressed with his master plan. The only condition of his release? Finishing the plan—every dream, every plan, every hope, every goal. He had to finish it all.

Newly free, Chris set out to do just that. When we met, he was running a social enterprise that employed other returning citizens in construction and the trades. When Bernie's film crew set out to film my story, Chris soaked it all up. I encouraged the campaign to tell Chris's story.

I could see flashes of fear when I first broached the topic with the campaign staff. Their eyes said it all: "Willie Horton." Decades earlier, then Vice President George H. W. Bush used images of Willie Horton, a convicted rapist turned murderer, to scare voters into electing him instead of the Democrat, Michael Dukakis. The Willie Horton ads would go down as one of the most effective and cynical dog whistles in the history of American politics.

I didn't push it. The campaign was already swamped, and before long my attention was completely focused on helping Bernie win—first in New Hampshire, where we announced my endorsement, followed by states around the country where I could help the campaign reach Black voters.

A few months later, as Bernie made ending mass incarceration a bigger, more prominent part of his campaign, I revisited the suggestion of telling Chris's story.

This time, Jeff Weaver, Bernie's campaign manager, was quick to respond. "We're one step ahead of you." The campaign was back in Baltimore filming Chris's story. Chris spoke from the heart and shared this:

> I've spent almost half of my life in prison, so sixteen years. I was always a dreamer. I used to go to the library all the time and read, and I would imagine a different world. I was able to mentally leave my neighborhood through reading. Growing up, I ran track, played chess. I played the cello at some point. I was raised in a very violent neighborhood. Every couple of months, we had to go bury somebody. My brother was shot. My cousin was gunned down right behind my house. I lost five friends before the age of seventeen. In my teenage years, my mom went through a terrible relationship with a police officer who sexually assaulted my mom, punched me, or pulled out his gun and put it to my head. I started carrying a weapon for protection. After so many times of him smacking my mom around, at some point, the next person that does something to me, I am going to respond. Not too long after that, people came after me, and I ended up taking a person's life. I felt terrible. It was hard for me to imagine that I did it. I was seventeen. My mustache had just grown in. They sentenced me to natural life in prison. I remember them putting me in a dark van. They just drove me away. I just came to the realization that I would probably never get out. That I would have to grow old and die here. My family stopped accepting my calls, and I wasn't getting visits from them. The mail stopped coming.
>
> I knew in my heart that I was a good person. I just decided that I wanted to turn my life around, and so I just started writing up a plan. Embracing my education could be my way out of prison. I called

it a positive delusion. I had to delude myself to believe that I could get out somehow. It allowed me to get up every day, and work really hard and study. And really embrace it. I became a mentor. I started volunteering. I started to help folks, and I just never stopped. When I wrote the master plan up, I sent a copy of it to my judge. Ten years had gone by and the judge says, "I will let you out but you have to finish your master plan.[1]

The campaign ad with Chris became the most successful of the 2016 Democratic Primary. It reached almost one million views the first day it was posted online. The ad was so popular that several political analysts estimated that if we had released it just a few weeks sooner, Bernie would have won Illinois. It proved that our political system's long-standing fear of ending mass incarceration is unfounded. While Willie Horton and Chris Wilson are both dark-skinned Black men convicted of deeply serious crimes, nevertheless Chris's story resonated with a broad base of the electorate. By centering Chris's humanity, the Sanders campaign broke through on the issue of criminal justice—the inverse of how the Bush campaign dehumanized and scared the electorate through the story of Willie Horton. Chris's story teaches us a lesson about the power of putting humanity at work to bridge our differences and make progress together.

( )

"Bernie Sanders just beat Hillary by seven points in the Michigan primary. The pollster said he'd lose by two. The same pollster says she'll beat Trump here by seven next fall." After typing that message, I added the emoji for fear, the one with the big eyes who looks terrified. I sent the tweet and boarded the plane.

A couple hours later, we touched down in Missouri. I looked out the window. There wasn't a three-story building in sight.

"Hey, y'all! Where are we?"

"We're in the Ozarks, Ben," answered Bernie's campaign manager, Jeff Weaver, in his trade-mark deadpan.

The answer surprised me as much as the scenery. For months, I'd been doing what retired Black civil rights leaders do on presidential campaigns, running my mouth and campaigning in South Carolina, Maryland, Illinois, and Michigan.

We had just won the Michigan primary. It was the first time a Jewish candidate had won. We won the majority of the Muslim vote. Our coalition was beautiful and we had the young of every color, gender, and faith. It was a beautiful rainbow that seemed to stretch far into the future.

Presidential campaigns are relentless in their pragmatism. Winning Michigan just meant we had the right to go fight in Missouri with hope. It also meant that new donations would come flowing in. Our greatest strategic constraint was that we only had money about two weeks before we needed it. We weren't bundling big checks in back rooms or fancy parlors. We were bundling small checks through the internet and the waves became tsunamis only when a victory happened.

Right now, we were on a high, and I was staring at the no-rise skyline, thinking I should have paid attention that they said Missour-uh, as opposed to Missour-ee. Missour-ee would have meant we were headed to where I thought we were headed, St. Louis or Kansas City, the urban hubs of the state, the places where I could be maximally helpful. Missour-uh, on the other hand, was the rest of the state.

And here we were.

"What time y'all going to be back? St. Louis is next, right?" I queried, still hoping I could stay put.

"Yeah, Ben, St. Louis is next, but you need to get off the plane."

"I'm cool, Jeff. I'll just hang out here and read."

"No, Ben, we need you tonight. You need to get off the plane for real, for real."

"All right."

I stepped off the plane and hopped in the car. We sped to the university. Cornfields and forests, beautiful. I still wasn't sure why they needed me. We rolled into the Southwest Missouri State University campus. It looked a little bit like Detroit. It looked a little bit like Chicago. There were 7,000 people outside hoping to get in. The fire marshal was telling them, no, the place was full. There were 5,000 more inside. And yet again, Bernie and I were both grumbling, two old organizers confounded as to why folks would not anticipate that we would have a crowd at least twice as large as any venue we were in and be ready with the system. Once again, we were scrambling. The team was doing a great job, but truly, this situation should have been anticipated.

We made our way inside. I poked my head through the curtains. The crowd inside was different than the crowd outside. Apparently, the locals had shown up early. Outside, there were university students, bicycles and skateboards and backpacks. And inside, it appeared that half the men were in deer hunting camouflage. This was a homegrown Ozarks crowd. "Who's bringing out Bernie tonight?"

"You are, Ben."

"Ha, ha. Don't fuck with me, Jeff. I'm too tired for that shit. Who's bringing out Bernie tonight?"

"You are, Ben." Jeff wasn't joking.

"You all think they want to hear from me, the former head of the NAACP? This crowd?"

"Ben, they'll eat it up. Just watch."

"Okay, Jeff."

( )

My mama raised me with one repeated instruction: Do something that scares you every day. I knew what that was going to be tonight. I stepped out onto the stage and gave my stump speech for Bernie. It was all about the threat of Donald Trump. In March, a full two months before George Stephanopoulos would ridicule Keith Ellison on national television for merely suggesting that Donald Trump might win the Republican primary.

But this crowd got it. I mean they loved their neighbors, but the neighbors also apparently scared them a little. When I rolled into my speech, when I tore into Donald Trump, they erupted. They understood the threat. They felt his divisive movement building all around them. And they knew the only antidote was a unifying populist movement.

And then I brought out Bernie and I did something you don't always do when you're traveling with Bernie from coast to coast. I stayed to listen to the entire speech again. Bernie's speech is like the song "Free Bird." It's long, and everybody has a favorite line. And if they're drunk or a little overexcited, they will scream out their favorite line at exactly the wrong time. If you're a surrogate, or a staffer, if you're focused on winning, the best thing you can do when Bernie is giving the speech is get in a back room or head back to the hotel and sit down and figure out how you're going to win bigger tomorrow. But tonight, I wanted to hear Bernie's speech from beginning to end.

You see, I was down for *these people*. But I needed to know they were down for *my people*. At a certain point, Bernie's speech becomes a policy statement. He recites each of the things he plans to change. I was there specifically to hear how the crowd would respond when Bernie put out the call for the police to stop killing unarmed Black women and unarmed Black men.

As we approached that point of the speech, I stopped breathing. I knew how the crowds in Detroit and Chicago had responded. In Chicago, they were reeling from the revelation that the mayor, Rahm Emanuel, had hidden the police execution of Laquan McDonald in order to secure his reelection. In Detroit, they had been tortured, literally tortured by the police for decades, as they had been in Chicago too.

I held my breath. I closed my eyes and then Bernie made the call and the crowd erupted as loud as maybe louder than in Detroit and Chicago.

I ran to the curtains. I pushed my head through. There were men in deer-hunting camouflage who had jumped into their seats, thrown their fists in the air, and were hollering. I thought they must holler only in the Ozarks. Suddenly it hit me. We all had issues with Boss Hogg. There was a reason my cousins in West Baltimore loved the 1980s television show the *The Dukes of Hazzard* so much. Bo and Luke Duke were always fighting Boss Hogg. There was no one more corrupt or unjust in all of Hazzard County.

Tears rolled down my cheeks at the sight of all those White Ozarks locals roaring in solidarity about the need to stop the killing of unarmed Black people. There was hope for our country, hope that we would achieve Frederick Douglass's vision for America's destiny, even sooner than I had thought possible.

21

RISING UP TOGETHER

Huh," she said, as if nothing in her life had prepared her to hear a White man, let alone a Republican, describe Black American children as "our kids."

It was the summer of 2001, and I was in Los Angeles at the invitation of my friend John Bryant, the founder of Operation HOPE. He had convened leaders from across the country to discuss the way forward for our nation on the occasion of the tenth anniversary of the riots that burned Los Angeles after four White officers were acquitted of the savage beating of a Black motorist named Rodney King.

I was waiting in the wings, preparing to go on stage and deliver my speech.

At the lectern addressing the gathered crowd was Congressman Jack Kemp. "Our kids! Our kids! Our kids!," he yelled, pounding on the lectern. He was on fire about the undereducation of Black children, the stealing of their financial futures, the need for us as a nation to recognize that all our kids are all our kids.

An elder stateswoman of South Central LA, who stood next to me, leaned over and said, "Where is he from?" I said, "Ma'am, that's Jack Kemp. The congressman. The one who ran for president as a Republican."

"I know who he is, *boy*. Where. Is. He. FROM?"

I stared at her for a moment, my mind racing for the answer.

She raised her eyebrows for emphasis.

"New York, ma'am. I believe he's from upstate New York."

"Huh? Then whose kids is he talking 'bout?"

I did not just hear her confusion at the apparent contradiction, I felt it.

I looked at her with the empathy of someone who had lived in that space and said plainly, "I think his point is we are all Americans, they are all American children, and thus they are all 'our kids.'"

The notion stunned her.

Years later, I crossed paths with Jack again. Julian Bond named him as co-chair of the Commission on the Future of the NAACP. One of the first Black people elected to the Georgia legislature after the passage of the Voting Rights Act, Julian Bond was a notoriously progressive Democrat. He had a photograph of Dr. Martin Luther King Jr. standing next to him, casting a ballot in his first election.

He also was a profound student of history. He understood that people and parties change over time. One hundred years earlier, most Black folks were Republicans; today, most Black folks are Democrats. One hundred years earlier, most White men were Democrats; today, most White men are Republicans. He also understood that it was even more important that one's party affiliation represented one's core beliefs and priorities, and that one's principles, and one's basic responsibilities to the family, the community, and the country reign supreme.

In short, he understood, in his bones, that if we were actually going to succeed in making America an America for all of us—not just Black or White, or rich or poor, but of all colors and of all stations—then we would have to have the courage to extend the hand of friendship to everyone. As I learned in that Waffle House in Mississippi, it was the only way to find every American who deep in their hearts agreed with us on the need to achieve our national vision of being one nation— *E pluribus unum*, out of many, one.

Jack Kemp was a courageous man. He was also as plainspoken a man as I had ever met amongst the U.S. Congress. When he sought the Republican nomination for president, a reporter had cornered him and asked, "How can you be a Republican and a card-carrying member of the NAACP?"

The year was 1988. Twenty years earlier he had been a quarterback in the NFL in the years when the league was being integrated by the NAACP.

As he'd tell me years later, he answered the reporter by simply saying, "I can't help but care about the rights of the people I used to shower with."

No comeback to that. The reporter relented.

The force that drives us to recognize the human dignity of our fellow Americans, regardless of their color, ethnicity, or race, is a power older than our country itself. There is a gravity within humanity that pulls our hearts toward each other, despite demagogues, terrorists, or even governments trying to split us apart and pit us against each other. That gravitational pull helped power the uprisings in Gloucester. It rippled through the ink when my distant cousin President Thomas Jefferson penned the words, "We hold these truths to be self-evident, that all men are created equal, that they are endowed by their Creator with certain unalienable Rights, that among these are Life, Liberty and the pursuit of Happiness." And again when he confessed, "I tremble for my country when I reflect that God is just; that his justice cannot sleep forever."

That force united the men on the docks of Boston, who stood shoulder to shoulder as the Redcoats mowed five of them down.

That force motivated my grandma's grandfather when he helped lead former slaves and former Confederates to assert their rights, to assert their children's rights to a free education and their own rights to public higher education they could afford.

That force moved through the hand of the Rev. Dr. Martin Luther King Jr. as he finished his "Letter from Birmingham Jail" and handed it to a White prison guard he urged to join the civil rights movement because the guard was so deeply underpaid.

That force ordered the mind of Bob Zellner's father as he struggled for his own sanity. If we're honest, it's there in the hearts of each of us. It's in the pages of the parables you read in this book. I hope the lessons stick.

As a person of faith, I would say that force is divine. Julian Bond, who chose not to follow any religion and professed no belief in God, would say it's just people recognizing the logic that his old professor Dr. King taught him at Morehouse: it's always the right time to do the right thing. One thing we both agreed on is that all of us come into the world as close to perfect as possible. And yet we each are ultimately forced to choose whether we fight or submit to the insanity and lie that is racism. Racism and its legacy are impossible to escape in our nation, in the same way that it was impossible to escape the soot in the air of Pittsburgh when it was a factory town. Overcoming that inheritance and building a stronger nation starts with each of us becoming more connected to our neighbors, those that are our family members, our friends, and ultimately, those who live on the other side of the tracks or the freeway or the invisible wall that is color in America.

As a Christian, I would urge every leader who shares my faith to courageously interrogate the dilemma of what Jesus would do, and then push themselves and their parties fearlessly to champion the poor and root out hate with love truly modeling themselves after the man they celebrate each Christmas. In short, it's time for us all to practice the Golden Rule. As Dr. King would remind us, it's central to all of the world's great religions. As Jesus himself reminded us, the person of no faith who follows the Golden Rule is more worthy than the person who proclaims to have great faith but fails to treat their neighbor as themself.

In one of the last conversations I had with Jack Kemp, we each reflected on our admiration for the timeless words of Dr. Martin Luther

King, and Frederick Douglass. Frederick Douglass was a light for King, in the way King is a light for many today. Douglass championed the notion of a big America that does not fear immigrants but welcomes them recognizing that they come here because of our strength and seeking to add to it. A big America where our color would not divide us but our humanity unite us. A big America where we recognize it will take all of us to achieve our nation's greatness. A big America where no one would be a servant or slave, and everyone would have the opportunity to succeed and to dream that their children might succeed even higher.

He reflected on our nation's unique mission in the world. He pointed to world-connecting geography: we are bordered by great nations, north and south, defined by people of different colors and languages. We are bordered by great oceans east and west that connect us to every people on the planet. He reflected on our nation's character, defined as that nation at its best, not its worst. When a person acts badly, we say that they're acting outside of their character. So it is for nations too.

Douglass pointed to a powerful economy and our limitless potential. And nineteenth-century America's great and peaceful warrior hero bellowed that "America's mission" was to be "the most perfect national illustration of the unity and dignity of the human family that the world has ever seen."

Jack Kemp believed that was our mission too. I do as well. That mission is bigger than any party, any community, or any individual. And yet the only way we'll achieve it is if we humble ourselves to work on ourselves, to work courageously in our communities, and to commit to cross all the lines that have historically divided us.

As a Jewish rabbi fated for execution by an emperor's henchman told his followers two millennia ago, it's time for us to love our neighbors as ourselves. And like the Good Samaritan on that road to Jericho, we must recognize our neighbors aren't simply the ones who look like us, but they are also the ones in the ditch. And as a wise former Ku Klux Klansman noted, we are all down here in this ditch together.

When my great-great-grandfather Edward David Bland, the son of a man kept as a slave by his own brother, found himself in that ditch, he realized his only way out was to follow the Golden Rule, which unites all the world's great faiths. He ultimately recognized that we are all God's children and practiced the grace his father preached. In the process, he truly became his brother's keeper.

The multiracial populist movement built by Edward David Bland and General Mahone lasted only a few years. Still, their coalition—and similar ones in other states at that time—laid the groundwork for the New Deal and War on Poverty coalitions that rose up in the twentieth century. their legacy of free public education and great public universities endures in the twenty-first. And yet and still, they remind us that the spirit of the rebels in Gloucester does as well.

As I write these words, my grandma is weak and tired. She is 105 and dying in the medical wing of her retirement home. So I will say it here for her as I will say it one day to my own grandchildren: "Never forget our people were always free." Never forget, when it comes to building an America as good as her promise, we the people are always more powerful than we think we are.[1]

AN OPTIMIST'S GREATEST GIFT

My grandmother died at 105, just as I finished this book. Writing it was my last great gift to her as it assures her wisdom will live on with future generations. It captures her stories, her aspirations for our nation, her sensibility, and her values. All of those have been a great gift to me, my parents, my sister, and our kids. They are now our gift to you. You may have noticed that one of the defining traits my grandmother received from her grandfather Edward David Bland is her optimism. It is the source of both her resilience and ours as a family.

Two months before my grandma died, Barbara Mikulski called her. As often happens with our mentees, the senator has been my grandmother's hero for decades, and yet my grandmother is still a hero to her. When I met the senator at a women's political event, she walked up to me and asked if I was Mamie Todd's grandson. When I told her that I was, tears ran down her cheeks. Knowing the love they share for each other, I asked the senator if we could three-way telephone my grandmother's medical unit at her retirement home.

Once we were all on the phone, Senator Mikulski eulogized my grandmother to my grandmother. "Mamie, you are a national legend in child protection. Do you remember how they treated those kids down at the jail before we did what we did?"

I didn't know exactly what they were talking about, but figured it had something to do with my grandmother's role in helping to launch Child Protective Services in Baltimore. She made a name for herself shortly after returning to Baltimore after graduating from the University of Pennsylvania School of Social Work, having attended that Ivy League university because the state of Maryland paid for her to do so. A decade earlier, Thurgood Marshall won a discrimination lawsuit lodged against him on behalf of the state's aspiring Black graduate students.

The courts found that Maryland had failed to make sufficient provision to educate Blacks aiming for graduate degrees. Therefore, the state needed to create a scholarship to send them out of state. My grandmother figured the state wanted them to remain out of state. She would give them no such pleasure. She commuted to the University of Pennsylvania in Philadelphia from the tenements of West Baltimore, shepherded to and fro by my grandfather's former colleagues on the railroad.

When she finished her education, she launched a crusade against clubs frequented by the wealthiest men in town. These clubs existed largely to facilitate the sexual exploitation of Baltimore's most vulnerable children.

My concern about the urgent need to improve the welfare of all our children is rooted in a strong desire to remove the barriers facing them and to ensure that their parents have a fair shot so that they have a fair shot. That concern comes from my grandmother. I inherited it from her like she inherited it from her grandfather. He built a populist movement in Virginia. She helped lead the war on poverty in Maryland, crisscrossing the state as the head of social policy implementation for what was then the Maryland equivalent of the federal Department of Health,

Education, and Welfare. She told me stories about dealing with issues of water quality in Appalachia. She worked so that every kid's parent could earn a decent living. She fought to make sure that the children in the poorest parts of the state, whether they lived in urban or rural communities, or were Black or White, all enjoyed a quality education.

I often think of her when I cross through Appalachia. In so many ways, Appalachia is a window into the soul of our country.

Once, I got lost in a holler and ended up in a local store asking for directions. The gas pump looked like it had been borrowed from the Smithsonian, a testament to the power of poverty as a force of historic preservation. It was still in operation, yet I had no idea how to operate it. Fortunately, I had gas in my tank. I just needed directions. I stepped into the store. The man at the counter was framed by bottles on a narrow shelf behind him, each with a different pickled part of a pig. The eyeball in a jar staring back at me caught my attention.

I considered the Confederate flag on his hat. It's common in the region but his hair was curlier than mine, his nose was just as broad, and he was darker. I started to ask him about his heritage but I stopped. I knew I was staring at the face of a man who was from what the local people referred to as the Melungeon. The Melungeon claimed to have descended from the Portuguese. The historian Henry Louis Gates Jr. ultimately convinced them to let him analyze their DNA in order to prove their Portuguese lineage. As I suspected, and Dr. Gates suspected and then confirmed, the Melungeon were simply the descendants of runaway slaves and British settlers. Among them, no doubt, if you go back far enough, you'll find many a runaway indentured servant, too.

The face of the Melungeon is like the cultural face of the region, it's like bluegrass music. It presents itself as Whiter than White. But all you have to do is stare at it for only a moment, and its African roots are more than clear. The banjo, West African. The jaw harp, brought over by West African slaves. The washtub bass, West African too. The melodies, many of those West African as well. The hollering, the moaning, the sighing, all typical of West African music. And bluegrass, bluegrass is like America: rebellious, European, African, and undeniably American all at once.

I believe that we can ultimately be as in rhythm with one another as the musicians in any bluegrass band, weaving all of that European heritage, all of that African heritage, hints of Native American heritage, all together at once. Heck, the mouth harp ultimately goes back to Asia. We can be that "perfect example of the unity and dignity of the human family" that Frederick Douglass envisioned a century and a half ago. We've already achieved it in music in so many ways. And not just in bluegrass but in rock 'n' roll, soul, R&B, country, and jazz. The music that defines our nation, all of it, is gospel, which is the harmony of all of us—of all of our traditions. A piano here, a banjo there, a West African rhythm here, a European melody there, all blended together. Hints of Asia and other places woven through. Native American drums. Jewish klezmer. It's all right there.

Like my grandmother, I believe that we can rediscover the solidarity that America's working people knew in the Virginia colony's earliest days before notions of race were used to sow deep political divisions. We can remember that we are all concerned about the future of all our children. We can rise up together to demand freedom on behalf of all our children.

But first we have to start by listening to one another.

And as we do, we must speak freely from our hearts in the languages that tend to pull on the heart strings and unite most Americans. When we do so, we speak in terms of the values that unite our faiths (and people of goodwill who aren't believers), the love we share for our neighbors and families, our abiding patriotism and belief that our nation has a great destiny, and the great American Dream that our children will be better off than us. In the process, we remind ourselves that even bigger than our own families there is a great American family to which we all belong. Faith, Love, Patriotism, Aspiration, are the love languages of the American heart. Look back at the speeches of FDR and Eleanor Roosevelt or MLK and Coretta Scott King, and you will see them all there. Same for the speeches of Frederick Douglass, Barbara Jordan, and Jack Kemp. Ronald Reagan, when he was at his best, spoke this way too.

Early on in her career, my grandmother's courage won her a coterie of young admirers among the state's aspiring social workers. Six decades ago, one of those admirers was a young social work student named Barbara Mikulski. You could feel the mutual admiration in their conversation.

As they bantered back and forth on phone, you could feel the bond between them became very clear. One had grown up in the toughest parts of South Baltimore and carried that accent like a badge of honor. The other had lived with her husband and raised her daughter in segregated public housing in West Baltimore. They were proud of their accomplishments and shared a hard-earned loathing for business-as-usual at the state capitol. (My grandmother once told me she was the first Black woman to have a personal parking spot at the Maryland State Capitol. It was a necessity because the police were so baffled by a Black woman repeatedly parking there that they frequently questioned her right to do so. The governor put her name on the parking space to stop the problem.)

As I listened to these two senior stateswomen talk, I couldn't help but notice the lightness in their voice, their happy warrior demeanor. We live in such hard times, such fraught times, and yet the two of them remained determined and, ultimately, so positive.

I confronted my grandmother about her optimism once when I was young. My days in New York had made me jaded. I adopted the posture of always being concerned, stressed, earnest, dour. The world was so hard. The struggle was so hard. Stakes were so high. How could somebody be so lighthearted and positive? Didn't my grandmother know how much was wrong in the world? She spent her whole life in the struggle. She looked at me and she said, "Baby, it's true. Pessimists are right more often, but optimists win more often. In this life, you have to decide what's more important to you. As for me"—she smiled—"I'll take winning."

ACKNOWLEDGMENTS

In 1776, seven of my ancestors were on the battlefields of Massachusetts fighting for freedom, one was just fifteen with a fife and a musket. A little less than a century later, two of my ancestors born into slavery in Virginia rose to be state legislators and helped rebuild and reshape the Commonwealth after the Civil War. This book is in the spirit of their and their families' collective determination to build a nation that can deliver the "blessings of liberty" to all its children.

I'm grateful for my family: my brilliant, beautiful, and courageous children, Morgan and Jack; my sister, brother-in-law, and niece, Lara, Ike, and Nina; my parents, Ann and Fred; my late grandparents, Annette, Sargent, Mamie, and Jerome; Cecelia, Sharon, and Lia Epperson; Christopher John Farley, and my niece and nephew Emma and Dylan Farley; Lewis Goldfrank; Andrew Bundy; my late godfather, Bill Chappelle, my godsiblings Felicia, Yussuf, and Dave, and their children and spouses for enriching my life, inspiring me, making me laugh, giving me hope, and just making life more fun, even through grueling tasks like finishing your first full-length narrative manuscript; my godbrother Patrick Brice, his wife Lynsay, and children Otto and Anja; the surrogate mothers who helped raise me, Judy, Valerie, Lillian, Louise, and Bettina; my uncles from New England, Jim, who passed while I was completing this book, and Bill and his wife Jonnie, for always being there whenever I call; my Jealous cousins, Marnie, John, and Heather, for enriching my childhood and my life; and my cousin Scott Jealous for keeping me laughing, even as his husband fights cancer. I also want to appreciate my dozens of cousins in Virginia and Maryland—the Blands, Baughs, Johnsons, Williamses, and Stricklands and the extended Morgan, Roberts, and Rawlings families for filling my life with laughter, inspiration, and storytelling.

Beyond my parents' and grandparents' house, my faith was cultivated by my church family at St. James' Episcopal Church in West Baltimore, where I, like my mother, was baptized, and in Episcopal and Anglican institutions in Maryland, Virginia, New York, California, and England, including St. James', St. Mary's Manhattanville, and the York School, Columbia University, and Oxford University. I am especially indebted to the late Father Tabb, the late Father Castle, the late Canon Williams, Father Starr, Father Kooperkamp, Father Meadows, Father Truiett, and the active members of the Mamie and Jerome Todd Outreach Ministry of St. James' Church.

I'm inspired every day by my colleagues at People for the American Way, including our members and our fearless leader, Norman Lear—full of energy, even though he is now more than 100 years old—his wife Lyn, his family, and his team at Act III: Brent Miller, Cindy Villa, and Liana Schwarz. I also want to thank the board and the staff and call out a few of the many great women who have joined Norman as builders of this organization: the late Barbara Jordan, Kathleen Turner, Mary Frances Berry, and Dolores Huerta. They each inspire me to live a life of courage and candor. I especially wanted to thank Peter Montgomery for leaning in to help me edit this book in the middle of his full-time workload at the organization, as well as the team of leaders with whom I work closely every day. I am indebted to Na Eng and the communications team. I also want to express my deep gratitude for our board leadership, including Lara Bergthold, Reverend Tim McDonald, Cookie

Parker, David Altschul, and Greg Frezados, as well as our staff leadership Marge Baker, Svante Myrick, Diane Laviolette, Kristen Smith, Elise Convy, Roger Vann, Raquel Jones, and Damon Lipscomb. I am also grateful for the friendship of the incomparable Mark E. Pollack.

I am grateful to the University of Pennsylvania, and specifically the Annenberg School of Communication, the Carey Law School, the School of Social Policy and Social Practice, and the Africana Studies Department, for their encouragement. And in completing this book, I'm grateful for the deans of those schools, John Jackson, Ted Ruger, and Sally Bachman, who have been great friends to me as I have found my footing as a professor and for their partnership in the work of training the next generation of young leaders. I am grateful to the chair of the Africana Studies Department, Camille Charles, for her guidance and patience as I finished this work. I am also deeply appreciative of Kristen de Paor of SP2 for her encouragement and support throughout the process. I also want to thank Corina Scott, Alison Harik, Ben Wrobel, and Maria Quintero for their intrepid assistance with the research for this book and their persistence in helping me move forward in producing it.

This project has had many stops and starts. I cannot overstate enough the role of Fagan Harris in encouraging me to continue and helping me to organize for and execute its completion. You have been my friend and brother for many years, and we have done great things together, more than once, and I look forward to many decades more. Thanks, too, to your incomparable wife Meryam Bouadjemi for her endless patience.

This book would not have been possible without the early guidance, encouragement, counsel, and hard work of Peter McGuigan, Tiffanie Drayton, Bret Witter, and Tracy Sherrod, as well as our team at HarperCollins and Amistad, including Patrik Bass, Judith Curr, Stephen Brayda, Francesca Walker, and Alexa Allen. Nor would much of it have been possible without the research of Dr. Henry Louis Gates Jr. and his colleagues including Nick Sheedy and the legendary late Johni Cerny.

I also appreciate the promotional efforts of Justin Loeber at Mouth Digital, as well as Theo Moll and Ronda Estridge at Keppler Speakers.

I am always indebted to my civil and human rights family, the organizations of the Leadership Conference on Civil and Human Rights and its fearless leader Maya Wiley. The teams at Our Revolution, Progressive Maryland, CASA de Maryland, the League of Women Voters, Stand Up America, Black Voters Matter, the Workers Circle, the Rosenberg Foundation, the African-American Ministers Leadership Conference, Democracy Initiative, National Vote at Home Institute, National Popular Vote, *The Nation* magazine, Human Rights First, *Harper's Magazine*, *Lapham's Quarterly*, National Urban League, the National Coalition to Abolish the Death Penalty, Amnesty International, Golden State of Opportunity, Community Organized Response Effort (CORE), National Newspaper Publishers Association (NNPA), the NAACP Legal Defense Fund, SEIU, CWA, NEA, RWDSU, AFT, AFL-CIO, and most importantly, the National Association for the Advancement of Colored People (NAACP).

I'm honored to have served as the seventeenth president of the NAACP, serving its members alongside chairs Julian Bond and Roslyn Brock; grateful to have grown up in the movement alongside its current president Derrick Johnson and to have been counseled by Hazel Dukes, its current chairman Leon Russell, and many others; to have learned from Revs. Joseph Lowery, Al Sharpton, Amos Brown, and Jesse Jackson, as well as Marc Morial; to have been trained by many of the NAACP's most fearless members in Baltimore, New York, Mississippi, and Monterey County, California. I am proud that my family has belonged to the Association for six generations. May the tradition continue.

And I also want to thank the late Secretary Jack Kemp, Secretary Colin Powell, and the many conservative leaders who have been unexpected allies in moments of great consequence. Many of those moments are summarized in the book. I won't state them now. I am deeply grateful to Governor Bob McDonnell for his courage while in office, the unique level of commitment he showed in working with us, his friendship, and his ongoing leadership in increasing racial reconciliation in the Commonwealth of Virginia. I also want to express my appreciation to Grover Norquist, Newt Gingrich, Governor Arnold Schwarzenegger, Governor Rick Perry, Governor Nathan Deal, and former Lieutenant Governor Michael Steele for stepping up in ways we did not expect during our NAACP drive to shrink prisons and increase justice in the American justice system.

While finishing this book, circumstances have prompted me to become even more engaged in the struggle to protect our environment and save our planet. I have deep gratitude for my friends at the Trust for Public Lands, the Wilderness Society, the Environmental Defense Fund, the National Audubon Society, and the Sierra Club.

My faith that what many considered to be impossible is not just possible, but achievable, was first stoked by my parents and grandparents, Black and White, who live lives of courage. In recent years, that faith has been accelerated by my involvement in a community of innovators who are committed to finding and building companies that make the world better in ways that are meaningful and palpable. I want to thank Mitch and Freada Kapor for bringing me into their community, and my former colleagues at the Kapor Center for leading me into this work. I am grateful to my colleagues on the board of Pigeonly, Aspiration, Luminary, and Curve Health, as well as my friends at Basic Power and Citizen who both inspired and challenged me and were patient with me in the years I was writing this book. I also want to thank the many creatives and innovators who inspired me as I was completing this book, including Joe Sanberg, Soleiel Moonfrye, Rosario Dawson, Andrew Frame, Prem Akkaraju, Erik Moore, Arthi Shahani, Mike Sepso, Chloe Flower Frederick Hutson, Jotaka Eaddy, Charles Hudson, James White, Jackson Gates, Brian Dixon, Fatma Ismail, Rishi Malhotra, Patrick Gaston, Andrei Cherney, Ulili Onavakpuri, Steve Phillips, Lateefah Simon, Yasiin Bey, Nika Soon-Shiong, Ibrahim AlHusseini, Nate Redmond, Helen Melluish,

Tim Peck, Todd Park, Lisa Jackson, Rob Mac Naughton, Charlene Lake, Rosario Dawson, Troy and Rebecca Carter, Jay and Kawanna Brown, Rachel Maddow, Alyssa Milano, Charles Phillips, Lawrence Bender, Phillip Watson, the team at Appian Way, Steve McKeever, Jess Garner, Jalil White,Walter Skayhan, Gene Ostendorf, Wes Moore, Chris Wilson, Joey Hundert, Fatima Loeliger, Rick Segal, Alec Baldwin, Phaedra Ellis-Lampkins, Elie Mystal, Bradley Horowitz, Sam Brin, Roger McNamee, Wayne Jordan, Tim Silard, Gigi Dixon, David Drummond, Maurice Coleman, Sean Rad, Hill Harper, Harry Lennix, Cenk Uygar, Ellen Pao, Talib Kweli, Sean Penn, Dan Levitan, Will Carey, Ann Lee, Vicangelo Bulluck, Chad Vann, Danny Shader, Mike Seibel, Robert Mailer Anderson, and Bryonn Bain.

I also want to thank many old friends who counseled me and inspired me to keep pushing through the COVID-19 crisis to get this done, including Phil Radford, Josh Civin, Al Dwoskin, Steve Silberstein, Bernie and Jane Sanders, Leon and Sylvia Panetta, April Ryan, Virginia Kase Solomon, Jeff Weaver, Larry Cohen, Bishop Jamal Bryant, Fatma Ismail, Bishop William Barber, Steve Hawkins, Moneese DeLara, Rev. David Anderson, Robert Mailer Anderson and Nicola Miner, Quinn Delaey, Kweli Washington, Stacey Abrams, Amy Goodman, Clara Shin, Rachelle Bland, Rabbi David Saperstein, Van Jones, Hassan Murphy, Billy Murphy, Kevin Johnson, Zach McDaniels, Mike Rozen, Will Zerhouni, Ian Martin, Michael Parrish, Rene Spellman, Sam and Shary Farr, Steve Miller, Charles Phillips, Ally Sheedy, Cory Booker, Nina Turner, Cam Cowan, John Hope Bryant, Alex Norton, Leah Hunt-Hendrix, Kevin Harris, Travis Tazelaar, Megan Nashban, Dwayne Proctor, Rob Speyer, Sam Campbell, Vakil and Shannon Smallen, Erica Bernstein, Tara Young, Bobby Bland, Lindi Von Miutus, John and Amy Underwood, April and Cliff Albright, Milan Reed, Russlyn Ali and Ben Littlejohn, Shefali Razdan Duggal, Eric and Amy Garcetti, Horacio Trujillo, Gina Kim, Bill Meyers, Joel Madden, Steve Fisher, Randa Serhan, Hank Torbert, Jason Small and Jumana Musa, Emerson and Danita Wickwire,

Vanessa Wruble, Andrea King and Martin Luther King III, Esther Benjamin, Kia Heath, Nancy Stephens, Bob Friedman, Tali Farhadian, Juan Williams, David and Masooda Young, Steve McKeever, Ana Yanez Correa, Sanjay Srivastava, David Smith, Timothy K. Lewis, Jason Morisette, Tom Layton and Gyongy Laky, Shauna Marshall, Len Riggio, Andy Shalal, Katrina Vanden Heuvel, Ken Sunshine, John Seifert, Andy Wong, Larry Stafford, Anthony Brown, Stuart Applebaum, George Gresham, Gerry Hudson, Cathy Hughes, Alfred Liggins, Wade Henderson, Hilary Shelton, Rodney Ellis, Jamie Raskin, Niaz Kasravi, Judith Russel, Paul Franzese, Robert Sigfried, Hazel Trice Edney, Chris Rock, Kelley Fahey, Jeff Santos, and Elly Tatum. Special appreciation to Jessica Vanessa da Silva for making sure I kept laughing during the hardest moments of composing this manuscript.

I also want to appreciate my brothers in Kappa Alpha Psi, Sigma Pi Phi, and BMe. My work as a leader and single parent often keeps me from meetings. However, I have never left the bond, and I always answer the call of any brother asking for assistance, and I always will.

Similarly, please let me thank Delta Sigma Theta, Virginia State University, the University of Pennsylvania, and the Pierians; the first three institutions shaped my beloved grandmother, Mamie Todd, and the last she helped to create.

Finally, I want to thank you, the reader. If you made it through this acknowledgments section, you've made it through the book. It was written with candor and in the same voice that I would use as if we were sitting together having a drink at my local bar. If I've never met you before, I hope to meet you one day along the journey that is building, maintaining, and realizing the promise of the greatest democracy the world has ever known. Let us all commit to live by the Golden Rule and extend the hand of friendship to all our neighbors with the faith that we have more in common than we don't: *E pluribus unum.*

NOTES

1: Trouble in the Air

1. Hebrews 11:1, King James Bible.

2: Who Is My Family?

1. Daniel J. Sharfstein, "Crossing the Color Line: Racial Migration and the One-Drop Rule, 1600–1860," *Minnesota Law Review* 91 (2007): 592, available at http://scholarship.law.vanderbilt.edu/faculty -publications/386.
2. *Finding Your Roots*, "The Jealous Family Freedom Papers," PBS video, 53 minutes, aired October 14, 2014, https://www.pbs.org/video/finding-your -roots-jealous-family-freedom-papers/.

4: Discovering the Roots of Race

1. *Loving v. Virginia*, Oyez, www.oyez.org/cases/1966/395, accessed May 11, 2022.
2. *Loving.*
3. Barbara J. Fields, "Slavery, Race and Ideology in the United States of America," *New Left Review*, no. 181 (May 1, 1990): 95.
4. Fields, "Slavery, Race and Ideology," 95.
5. A. Leon Higginbotham, "The Colonial Period," in *In the Matter of Color: Race and the American Legal Process* (Oxford: Oxford Univ. Press, 1978), 273.

6. *Washington Post*, https://www.washingtonpost.com/blogs/she-the-people /post/obama-descended-from-slave-ancestor-researchers-say/2012/07/30 /gJQAUw4BLX_blog.html.

5: Making It to Twenty-One

1. Frederick N. Rasmussen, "Rave Reviews for Meals Served in Dining Cars," *Baltimore Sun*, January 3, 2010, https://www.baltimoresun .com/maryland/bs-xpm-2010-01-03-bal-md-backstory03jan03 -story.html.

2. "One Million Black Families in the South Have Lost Their Farms," last modified October 11, 2019, Equal Justice Initiative, https://eji.org/news /one-million-Black-families-have-lost-their-farms/.

3. "13th Amendment to the U.S. Constitution: Abolition of Slavery (1865)," last modified May 10, 2022, https://www.archives.gov/milestone -documents/13th-amendment.

4. Brennan Center for Justice, "Voting Laws Roundup 2013," last modified December 19, 2013, https://www.brennancenter.org/our-work/research -reports/voting-laws-roundup-2013.

5. ACLU, "Cracks in the System: Twenty Years of the Unjust Federal Crack Cocaine Law," October 2006, https://www.aclu.org/other/cracks-system -20-years-unjust-federal-crack-cocaine-law.

7: The Personal Perils of Peacemaking

1. Mark Oliver, "Death by Tire Fire: A Brief History of 'Necklacing' in Apartheid South Africa," *All That's Interesting*, May 19, 2018, https://allthatsinteresting .com/necklacing.

2. Michael Parks, "Tutu Stops Mob from Burning Man to Death: South African Bishop Pushes Through Angry Blacks to Rescue Suspected Police Informer," *Los Angeles Times*, July 11, 1985, https://www.latimes.com /archives/la-xpm-1985-07-11-mn-8444-story.html.

9: A Pandemic Ignored

1. Margaret K. Lewis, "The Death Penalty: Cruel but Still Not Unusual," *The Diplomat*, May 4, 2014.

2. Amnesty International, "On the Wrong Side of History: Children and the Death Penalty in the USA," October 1998, https://www.amnesty.org/en /wp-content/uploads/2021/06/amr510581998en.pdf.

3. T. C. Antonucci and H. Akiyama, "An Examination of Sex Differences in Social Support among Older Men and Women," *Sex Roles* 17 (1987): 737–49, https://doi.org/10.1007/BF00287685.

4. Debra Vandervoort, "Social Isolation and Gender," *Current Psychology* 19 (2012): 229–36, doi:10.1007/s12144-000-1017-5.

5. Maurice C. Taylor, "Sex and Suicide: A Study of Female Labor Force Participation and Its Effects Upon Rates of Suicide" (PhD diss., Graduate College of Bowling Green State University, June 1978).

6. Mary C. Daly, Daniel J. Wilson, and Norman J. Johnson, "Relative Status and Well-Being: Evidence from U.S. Suicide Deaths," Federal Reserve Bank of San Francisco Working Paper #2007-12, 2007.

7. Thomas Thurnell-Read, "Open Arms: The Role of Pubs in Tackling Loneliness," Loughborough University, 2021, https://hdl.handle .net/2134/13663715.v1.

8. David C. Stolinsky, MD, "Homicide and Suicide in America, 1900–1998," *Medical Sentinel*, 2001.

11: A Forgotten History of Race

1. Barbara J. Fields, "Slavery, Race and Ideology in the United States of America," *New Left Review*, no. 181 (May 1, 1990): 95.

2. Fields, "Slavery, Race and Ideology," 95.

3. Howard Zinn, "Drawing the Color Line," ch. 1 in *A People's History of the United States* (New York: Harper & Row, 1990).

4. Zinn, "Drawing the Color Line."

5. Zinn, "Drawing the Color Line."

12: Politics and Betrayal in Black and White

1. John A. Powell, "Post Racialism or Targeted Universalism?" *Denver University Law Review*, 2009, https://www.ohchr.org/sites/default/files /Documents/HRBodies/HRCouncil/MinorityIssues/Session3/statements /PostRacialismTargetedUniversalismbyJohnPowell.pdf.

2. Frederick Douglass, letter to William Lloyd Garrison, September 29, 1845, https://glc.yale.edu/letter-william-lloyd-garrison-september -29-1845.

3. "Financial Panic of 1873," United States Treasury, https://home.treasury .gov/about/history/freedmans-bank-building/financial-panic-of-1873.

4. "Financial Panic of 1873."

5. W. T. Clark et al., *Coalition Rule in Danville—the Danville Circular,* October 1883, Broadside1882.S89 FF, Special Collections, Library of Virginia, Richmond.

6. Clark et al., *Coalition Rule in Danville.*

7. Clark et al., *Coalition Rule in Danville.*

8. "Carter Glass (1858–1946)," contributor: Ronald L. Heinemann, https://encyclopediavirginia.org/entries/glass-carter-1858-1946/.

9. "Carter Glass (1858–1946)."

14: One in the White House, One Million or Two in the Big House

1. Errol Louis, "A Nod to History but the Focus Is on Today," *Daily News* (New York), July 17 2009, https://nydailynews.newspapers.com/image/572760970/?terms=Obama%27s%20most%20delirious&match=1.

2. Stephane Méchoulan, "The External Effects of Black Male Incarceration on Black Females," *University of Chicago Press Journals,* 2011, https://www.journals.uchicago.edu/doi/full/10.1086/656370.

3. Graham Boyd, "The Drug War Is the New Jim Crow," NACLA Report on the Americas, July/August 2001, https://www.aclu.org/other/drug-war-new-jim-crow.

4. Legislative Analyst's Office for the State of California, "Prisons vs. Universities Proposal Would Unwisely Lock Up Budget Flexibility," 2010, https://lao.ca.gov/reports/2010/edu/educ_prisons/educ_prisons_012610.aspx.

5. Legislative Analyst's Office for the State of California, "The Budget Package: 2011–12 California Spending Plan," 2011, https://lao.ca.gov/reports/2011/bud/spend_plan/spend_plan_081211.aspx.

17: The First State South of the Mason-Dixon

1. "Representation," Death Penalty Information Center, https://deathpenaltyinfo.org/policy-issues/death-penalty-representation.

19: An American Parable

1. Ann Todd Jealous and Caroline T. Haskell, *Combined Destinies* (Lincoln, NE: Univ. of Nebraska Press, 2013), ch. 3.

20: A Holler from the Hollers

1. "Be Bold, Change the System," campaign ad for Bernie Sanders for President, YouTube, https://www.youtube.com/watch?v=UUVmegV69og.

21: Rising Up Together

1. Inspired by a quote credited to Barbara Jordan, cofounder of People for the American Way: "What the people want is very simple—they want an America as good as its promise."